A Short Life

A SHORT LIFE

Jim Slotnick

ELM DRIVE PRESS, LOS ANGELES

Copyright © 1983 by Jim Slotnick; 2014 by Jon Slotnick and
Sara Jane Slotnick. All rights reserved. Published 2014.

Printed in the United States of America
11 12 13 14 15   2 3 4 5 6 7 8 9 10

ISBN 978-0-692-20550-1

Project Editors: Jon Slotnick and Beth Lieberman

Publisher's Cataloging-in-Publication
(Provided by Quality Books, Inc.)
Slotnick, Jim.
A short life/by Jim Slotnick.
pages cm
LCCN 2014941870
ISBN 9780692205501
SUMMARY: The unexpurgated memoirs of a young man
with cancer.

1. Slotnick, Jim. 2. Cancer–Patients–United States–Biography.
I. Title.

RC265.6.S568A3 2014   362.19699'40092
                      QBI14-600104

Elm Drive Press
137 N. Larchmont Boulevard, Suite 428
Los Angeles, California 90004

Dedicated to ...
mom and dad
sara and jon
joe and laurie

Contents

Foreword

THIRTY YEARS HAVE PASSED SINCE MY BROTHER Jim wrote this memoir, and it's been about that long since I picked it up to re-read it. I was with him for much of the time he was pounding it out on an ancient Olympia typewriter, lending a hand with a dab of Wite-Out or an occasional editorial comment, along with his girlfriend Laurie. So, by the time he finished the manuscript—about 24 hours before he died—I was pretty familiar with what he wrote.

There have been many occasions since then that I've let my mind wander to the place Jim had been in, many times I've tried to put myself in his shoes. To be perfectly honest, it's a pretty overwhelming and even scary feeling—one that would recur periodically in my dreams, and still does. That's one reason I had studiously avoided immersing myself in this book again.

Now, after three decades, I'm absolutely awed by my brother's strength and courage in writing this. Creating *A Short Life* was his outlet for expressing the joy, pain, and flood of other emotions he was experiencing as his time on the planet was rapidly running out.

To me, Jim was always the kind of person who could pretty much do anything he set his mind to, and do it well. Whether it was playing the guitar, pitching a baseball, making films, or getting into medical school—he always had the intelligence and work ethic to make it happen.

A Short Life is a case in point. As you take a brief journey through Jim's earlier years, and finish up the trip with his battle against brain cancer, you're in the hands of a funny and poignant storyteller. In the process, he gives voice to many themes that are universal for most of us: stumbling through childhood and adolescence in search of an identity; early work experiences that help define what you do and don't want to do with your life; the gift, power, and pull of friends, family, and lovers. And finally, the challenge that every one of us will face eventually—mortality.

It's impossible for me not to feel a deep sense of loss regarding Jim's way too early death, especially after being lucky enough to experience the deepening richness of my own life with the passage of time—the joys and struggles of raising a family, adventures with friends, and so much more—along with a welcome sense of anticipation of so much more to come. That said, in revisiting the book after so long, it was a great way to rediscover so many of the things that made Jim the amazing person he was—not the least of which was how fully he appreciated the gift of life.

I know in my heart that neither sadness nor pity were the lasting feelings Jim wanted to convey to, or instill in, the reader. Instead, I'm sure he'd be thrilled that people have been inspired by both the way he lived and the way he died—happy to know that he made a real and positive difference with this extraordinary effort.

JON SLOTNICK

Dear Reader

I WANT TO WRITE A BOOK BEFORE I DIE THAT HAS a pulsebeat, that yawns and breathes and hisses and steams with the condensate of my life; some of its ups and downs and smiles and lies and twists and turns and ins and outs. What follows is the true story of my humble life. Most of it is written precisely as it happened. Some of it is a good approximation of what happened. And some of it is merely the product of my fertile, overheated brain.

I have heard it said that even though Mozart died at the tender age of thirty-two, it would take a music transcriptionist an estimated thirty-five years of around the clock work to simply copy all of the composer's music. I tell you this because I feel like the imaginary transcriptionist, feverishly setting down his music as the sand in the hourglass runs down. You see, I feel like I want to write my story for whomever chooses to read it before this cancer rots away what little is left of my poor addled brain. More on the cancer later.

I shall press on with the spirit of wild Jack Kerouac as my guide. He typed the original version of *On the Road* in ten days on a single continuous roll of butcher paper, while under the influence of amphetamines. Those of you who don't particularly like Kerouac will claim that the poor technique comes through in his writing, but technique is not my concern. Surely Kerouac wasn't the reincarnate Thomas Wolfe that he fancied himself to be, but his best books live and breathe and excited my mind and he talks about jazz music and America, and the motion of trains and hitch-hiking and friendship and pain and laughter and I hope that all of those things are in here as well.

CHAPTER ONE

Very Early Influences

MY EARLIEST MEMORY IS ONE OF STANDING IN front of a TV set in Buffalo, New York, my birthplace. I was probably fondling my penis at the time, a habit I would rediscover in early adolescence, with all the refinements that consistent practice tends to bring. Pictures of the period show me to be a happy, fat, cute-looking kid. My sister appeared about a year after I was born. We are generally photographed together.

She was also a happy, fat, cute-looking kid, with a face like a little button and a short pixie haircut. I must have loved her as dearly then as I do now, judging from all of the pictures that show us eating, playing, sleeping, and bathing together.

When I was two years old, my family moved to Gainesville, Florida. I remember a beautiful weeping willow tree in our new backyard. I remember my dad and me playing catch with an old softball. I also remember biting the finger of one of my teachers who was scolding me, digit extended, for being too noisy in line.

I liked Florida a lot. We stayed there a number of years. I had a friend named Dan. We used to go out into the woods near his house and shit together. My parents lived right across the street from a Holiday Inn. A nice lady there taught me how to swim. The morning we left to move to Memphis, Tennessee, we visited the gift shop of the Holiday Inn. I was allowed to pick out a paperback for the ride. I chose a Western. I couldn't read much, but I liked the picture on the cover.

Once we settled into our house in Memphis, I lost no time establishing myself on my new block's social register. I started a dirt-clod fight with the slightly paunchy kid who lived across the street. His name was John Franklin and he quickly became my best friend. I loved to sleep over at his house. We would stay up late and read his many back issues of *Boy's Life* magazine. John also had a TV set in his own room. One time late at night we watched a fantastic Western in which the hero was tied between two wild horses by the bad guys. The bad guys tried to split the hero apart by whipping the horses.

At this point in my life I became aware that I was Jewish, and that most other people in my neighborhood were not. This realization wasn't based on any specific religious distinctions between the other kids and me. It came from a vague feeling of being slightly different. We were the only family in my neighborhood who owned a foreign car, didn't celebrate Christmas, and liked Kennedy in the 1960 election. These "cultural differences" set us apart from the mainstream far more than any specific religious beliefs or practices.

I was also one of the few kids on the block who wasn't a racist. I often heard my friends repeating the overtly racist dinner-table talk of their parents. My parents supported civil rights: they worked on a project that allowed black children in the Memphis school system to attend symphony concerts with the white kids. They told us never to use the word "nigger." But with the schizophrenic innocence of most liberals, they were perfectly happy to hire black maids—a procession of dirt-poor women who were constantly vilified at the dinner table for their ineptitude as domestic servants. I remember these women as middle-aged, but recently I had the opportunity to scrutinize some photographs of the period. The photos reveal them to have been no more than twenty years old.

This situation was difficult to sustain for any significant length of time. Yet my parents seemed puzzled as to why there was so much turnover in our domestic staff.

One day I remember answering the phone. Marvella was our maid at the time. "Hello?"

"Hello. Is Mrs. Slotnick at home?" the voice on the other end, clearly a black male, asked politely. I told him that I was the only person at home and offered to take a message for my mom.

"Just tell your mama that Marvella's husband called and that I don't want her cleaning no more white people's toilets!" Click.

In the early sixties, music stations were segregated. Black stations existed for black people, played black music, and used black actors and announcers to advertise their products.

Because I listened to whatever stations were set on the dial by the maid, I was exposed to blues, gospel, soul, and jazz music at an early age.

Aretha Franklin, B.B. King, Wilson Pickett, Marvin Gaye, Otis Redding: the musical distillate of the unnecessary pain and crap that results from living as a poor black in this country. Hearing this music back then made it easier for me to understand jazz later in my life. There is so much good music in the world of jazz: Miles, Bird, Monk, Trane, Hawk, and Diz to name a few—geniuses whose music burned a hole in my soul.

□

At this point in my life, baseball began to play a pivotal role. It was my best sport. I remember many muggy-warm Memphis nights when the neighborhood parents gathered to sip their after-dinner drinks on somebody's porch. John Franklin would be down in a crouch with his catcher's mitt on. I would be doing my best imitations of pitchers' windups that I had seen on television. I remember feeling a sense of power at being able to throw a baseball hard enough to sting somebody's hand.

Playing catch is such a beautiful, perfectly balanced ritual of give and take. POP! The ball is in your mitt. You remove it slowly. Without thinking about it you wrap your two longest fingers across the raised stitches on the cover of the ball.

Your left leg raises up, your body swivels on the right pivot and push-off foot, and the combined, properly coordinated, almost effortless actions of right hand, wrist, forearm, arm, shoulder, and trunk make the ball sizzle audibly as it zips toward the catcher. Slight pause while you wait for him to throw the ball back. POP! The ball is in your mitt. You make a nice, easy return toss. Pause. POP. Pause. POP. Pause. POP. Pause. On and on, over and over, until somebody loses the ball in the bushes, or dusk settles in with a cool breeze, or maybe someone's mom brings out iced tea in clear plastic cups that will be used later that night to catch fireflies.

Baseball is a wonderfully meditative game to play or watch. A friend of mine once told me that he loved to go to baseball games precisely for the reason that most critics of the game stay away: the lack of action. Most of a baseball game is devoted to waiting. Either the batter is waiting for the pitcher to throw, or the pitcher is waiting for the catcher to give him a sign, or the catcher is waiting for the runner at first base to take his lead. Consequently, the game lacks the dynamic pace of basketball and soccer or the repetitive intensity of football and boxing. In these sports, each explosive event is packaged into a "play" or a "round," surrounded by rest periods. Baseball games drift lazily along, just as when you're sitting by a stream watching it flow by. Sometimes you become aware that you're attending to the water itself, and sometimes you look up and it's the seventh inning already and it's been a pretty good game.

The nature of the sport offers the spectators plenty of time for fantasy and self-stimulation. In between the few moments of real action, the knowledgeable fan's mind can drift off into contemplation of the hitter's batting average or the state of the pitcher's fastball. A spectator may choose to ponder the condition of the shortstop's marriage or the condition of his own marriage. Then, all of a sudden, it's time for another pitch.

I love baseball because it is a game without the time limit associated with other sports. Hope can always spring eternal in the ardent fan's breast; there's always the bottom of the ninth; it's not over 'til it's over: there's always next year, a new spring season, new young men to play the game.

□

In Memphis, our neighborhood baseball games were highlighted by my friend Karl, who pitched for both sides. He also played quarterback for both teams whenever we organized a football game. There were two reasons for Karl's domination of the most prestigious positions in our games. First, he had the best arm on the block, and second, bone cancer was chewing away at his legs, confining him permanently to a wheelchair and preventing him from playing a position that required movement.

Karl was a very happy, friendly guy who never mentioned his health problems. He was phenomenally good at making plastic models. I would often go over to his house to shoot the breeze. I would sit for hours and watch him meticulously working away on a beautifully detailed replica of a World War I tank, or a modern Indy-racer, or an old sailing ship with all the rigging.

My dad worked as a bacteriologist at the hospital where Karl was being treated. One day, he came home after work to tell me that Karl had died. Dad, who had been with Karl's family at the end, said that my friend had been very calm and comfortable when it happened. He told me that Karl had probably felt like everybody else feels when they go to sleep. Except Karl wasn't going to wake up.

I didn't want to hear that my friend had gone and I couldn't believe that there wouldn't be any more wheelchair football games, or plastic models, or Karl's voice, or Karl's jokes, or Karl. No more Karl. How could he leave like that? I didn't care about the inevitability of his death, or about God, or leukemia, or any of that crap. I just wanted to catch a football from my friend in the wheelchair one more time.

A Short Life

I've lived with the possibility of my own death from cancer staring me in the face for two years and I still don't have any more rational or sophisticated ideas about the whole process than I did when Karl died. I'm curious as to what death is, but I know we'll all have the answer eventually, so I'm in no hurry to figure it out. Maybe it's nothingness, maybe it's fun, and maybe some intangible portion of Karl is communing with all the other "souls" that have held locker space here on earth. There is a part of me that ultimately feels so sad that Karl and I can't live forever, playing neighborhood games, watching TV, having fun, breathing, and being. But, given the opportunity, people would probably reject the prospect of immortality. Life is beautiful because it ends, not despite its finality.

Anyway, none of these are Karl's concerns right now. Wherever you are, Karl, I hope there are lots of models and glue and paints and decals and nice people to treat you right because you were a good guy and you deserve it.

□

Somewhere during this period of time I noticed that my brother had arrived on the scene. He was the cutest baby of the three kids and the only one of us who wasn't fat. In fact, he was a flat-looking baby. This earned him the nickname "Pompishka" (a variation on the Yiddish word for "pancake"). This would later become transformed into Pompee, Pomper, Pomp, etc. My brother would end up expending considerable energy during adolescence attempting to make the switch from "Pomp" to his real name, Jon, with all of the identity adjustments inherent in that transition.

I love my brother and sister tremendously. As a socialist I have no intellectual commitment to the concept of the nuclear family. I am saddened by most permutations of this institution that I have observed. I see the nuclear family as one of the key foundations of the patriarchal oppression of women in our society. I am amazed at the degree of individual alienation, pathology, and unhappiness that results from the power relationships existing between kids and parents. But, I must admit that I have been graced with a brother and a sister who, through two years of my cancer, have been strong, patient, open, and wise. They are unique characters. I feel that our hearts and souls and minds are clicking to the same beat. I suppose that in my version of socialism, the nuclear family can exist. For me, it's one option to be explored, but certainly not the only option.

In Memphis I made a startling political discovery of a different kind: the human species was divided into two different sexes. I remember my parents volunteering some reading material about this unexpected wrinkle, but I didn't get too much out of it. I relied on an alert empiricism to construct some semblance of a worldview on this subject. Unfortunately, my conception turned out to be an unhealthy and an all too typical, youthful misogyny. I hated girls and I would never, never, never get married— plain and simple.

The only girl I didn't hate was named Betsy P. I couldn't hate her because she was so cute, and short, very shy, and slightly plump. She had deep brown eyes and a ponytail. I displayed my love by completely ignoring her in class and on the playground. She was the one girl I never teased, chased, or threw the dodgeball at. I tried never to acknowledge her existence on the planet. At the same time, whenever she was around, I would indulge in the fantasy that she was watching my every move, and I would act as coolly as I could.

□

Our affair peaked one day in the cafeteria lunch line. Betsy's best friend, for whom I had absolutely no use, was a red-haired girl with a million freckles. She came right up to me and boldly asked if she could have "butts" in the line. I made it clear that I wasn't about to give up my place. She retaliated by trying to embarrass me. She asked loudly, "Are you Betsy's boyfriend?"

I remember saying, "Well, you'll just have to ask Betsy." A couple of minutes later I heard Betsy and her friend giggling in the back of the line. When I turned to look at what was going on, the red-haired girl said to me, "Betsy says she is your girlfriend!" Well, I guess that was as far as our relationship progressed. I don't ever remember seeing Betsy again. I don't remember walking her home, or talking to her alone, or calling her on the phone like some of my friends were starting to do with girls they liked. I wonder what happened to her.

I did a lot of fun stuff in Memphis. I remember this period of my life as being very happy. I remember going to school on mornings after it had rained and stepping on the long, red worms that had appeared on the sidewalk. I remember sliding into home plate with a home run just as my dad drove up from work in our old Rambler station wagon. I remember, one day after school let out, a teacher asking me how I had known what the word "perishable" meant. I placed second in the school spelling bee one year, and I had a friend who was locked out of his house for playing tennis with a black kid—and losing! I remember exchanging Christmas presents every year in school, and I remember the first overt infusion of politics into my life—the day JFK was murdered. School let out early that day and I felt uneasy about walking home without my parents. A friend of mine from Texas, whose parents never made him take a shower, said that it was probably a good thing that Kennedy was dead because "everybody knows that he was a nigger-lover." Then he went on about how good LBJ had been for Texas and what a great president he was going to be.

I remember peeing in my pants one day in front of my class while delivering a lecture on the Alamo. My poor teacher carefully asked me if I wanted to stop. I said it was okay, and continued on about Davey Crockett with a big pee stain running down my leg. Once, I got caught stealing baseball cards from the local drugstore. My dad used to yell at me all the time for my passive refusal to pick up the pinecones in the front yard (my first hostile reaction to arbitrary authority).

Occasionally I used to "camp out" in my pup tent and pajamas in the back yard. I grew a scallion garden with my friend John, but we never harvested it. One Halloween, a drunk lady put her pet kitten into my "Trick-or-Treat" bag.

Not necessarily anything too bizarre in these memories; a nice boyhood of basic Americana with the slight modulating influence of growing up Jewish in the middle of the southern United States. All in all, I liked Memphis, and the day we left for Los Angeles I was filled with nostalgia. I kept staring over and over at all of the faces in the picture of my fifth-grade class. I remember thinking how much I liked and would miss everybody and that I would come back and visit all the time. But for now, it was on to sunny California and the prospect of bigger and brighter things.

CHAPTER TWO

Healthy and Wealthy

THERE WAS NO WAY IN THE WORLD THAT AN eleven-year-old with my life experiences could be prepared for the culture of Beverly Hills, California. My folks thought that it was important for their kids to get a "good" education. The Beverly Hills public school system had been rated second in the country in a poll by one of the leading popular magazines. "So-we-loaded-up-the-truck, and we moved-to-Bev-er—leeee. Hills, that is, swimmin' pools, movie stars!"

The problem with growing up wild and free in the ghetto of Beverly Hills is that while the school system is excellent, the all-important socialization of a child takes place mostly outside of the classrooms. In school I was exposed to good intellectual opportunities. Outside of school I was faced with warding off the pernicious social values of the other kids.

When it came to finances, everyone else was in a different galaxy. We lived in the "slums" of Beverly Hills, three houses from the southern border with Los Angeles. Wilshire Boulevard, besides its importance as a famous and busy commercial roadway, played a major role in determining the Beverly Hills child's social status. As if just living in this city wasn't enough! Girls and boys living north of Wilshire, where the wealthier segment of the community lived, hung out with other boys and girls from north of Wilshire. The unfortunates who lived south of Wilshire could only mix socially with others who were similarly afflicted. Not only did my family live south of Wilshire, but also south of Olympic, and only one block from (egad) Pico Boulevard. Pico is a wonderful old street with good delis, Jewish bakeries, and failing businesses. It is not an impressive street to live near.

My address placed me into Beverly Vista Elementary School. B.V. was the most proletarian (I use the term loosely) of the city's four elementary schools. We even had a couple of token Mexican kids in our school. One of them, a cafeteria worker's son, was a friend of mine for a little while. I went over to his house once and his mom served us authentic Mexican tamales. I didn't know how to eat them. I began by trying to dissect and eat the cornhusk that they were served in, much to my friend's amusement. After lunch, we listened to a Rolling Stones album. I got into a big argument with my buddy. He kept showing me pictures of the Stones wearing sunglasses. My friend told me that the purpose of the glasses was to "hide their eyes, which are always bloodshot from smoking pot." I insisted that nobody could make music as good as the Stones if they were under the influence of marijuana.

In comparison to my moderate financial situation, the fiscal status of the kids I observed was impressive. Before coming to Beverly Hills I had never felt pinched for funds. I stole occasionally—more for the exotic thrill of getting something for nothing than out of necessity. However, I soon realized that my fifty cents a week wasn't going to keep me in a whole lot of Gucci tennis shoes. Some of the kids I hung out with seemed to have a fresh paper dollar every day!

I also had to adjust to the fact that the big game in this town was basketball. Back in Memphis, basketball had been considered a sport fit only for girls. Baseball ranked dead last in my new town. I was totally inept at basketball and self-conscious about it. Instead of shooting the ball during games and trying to improve my skills, I would unselfishly pass the ball to my teammates, work hard to rebound, play good defense, and generally run around the court making a lot of noise. My strategy paid off. I gained a reputation as a "hustler." The good basketball players let me play in their games and I became a moderately popular guy in my class.

□

Girls were a different story. I wasn't prepared on any level to deal with the opposite sex. I didn't realize it at the time, but neither was anybody else my age. I used to dread walking the three blocks to school in the morning because I would inevitably encounter Shelley and Lizzie on the way. I couldn't talk to them (!) so I had to ignore them—which was a ridiculous thing to do when they were only walking a few yards ahead of me. The three blocks began to feel like a marathon. I developed elaborate alternate routes to avoid these girls.

I wasn't any worse off than most of the other guys in my grade. I remember a few of my good friends referring to masturbation, so I figured it was alright that I was starting to do it. I had only a vague notion as to what "screwing" was. I knew with great assurance that it was bad to be a "fag." One day I wore a hand-me-down dress shirt my father had given to me. It had a little loop on the upper back. I was quickly assaulted on the playground by some asshole who ripped the loop (and the shirt) and yelled "fag-tag, fag-tag, fag-tag!"

About this time I met my friend Joe. In light of the fact that we have been best friends now for sixteen years, it is surprising to me that I can't remember how we met. I'm sure I first registered him when he threw me the ball during a basketball game, or while we were cheating off each other during a spelling test, or maybe one day after school, while he was walking home to his parents' apartment. We immediately became fast friends.

It's amazing to me now to think that two kids, so young and unformed, could choose each other as friends with such unerring accuracy; yet we did. Did I have any idea that Joe and I would go on to experience so much together? On some unconscious level I must have realized that there was something special about this guy. It was like the feeling of being at home, a commonality of thought and values that was as comfortable as a pair of worn-in sneakers. Joe possessed an ability to be loyal that bordered on the insane and marked him as a rare human being. Was it pure luck that the eleven-year-old kid I picked to be my buddy would be someone with whom I would share women problems, cancer, career ups and downs, death in the family, suicide attempts in the family, hitchhiking, socialism, Dodger games, and so much more? Joe would be important throughout my short life.

Other than my friendship with Joe, the bright spot in my life during this period was Little League baseball. Many of the hot-shot basketball players could hardly throw a baseball! My ability to play the game gave me the male peer respect that young boys crave. In my last year of Little League, I was good enough to make the All-Star team as a pitcher. I pitched in one game, struck out eleven batters in seven innings, had a three-hitter, and won 11-0. The other team was composed of bigger and tougher-looking kids. However, my catcher and I realized that these guys had probably never seen a curveball before. Every time I would get two strikes on one of their batters, I would throw my little dinky curveball right at his hip bone. The batter would bail out of the box to avoid getting hit and the slowly spinning ball would nip off the inside corner of the plate. Even if it didn't curve in for a strike, the batter would usually be so rattled by the experience that he would swing and miss at my next pitch—no matter what I threw. "Ste-e-e-e-rike THREE, you're OUT batter!"

That day remains one of the major highlights of my short life. It ranks on my list of personal achievements along with getting into medical school. I can still recall the feeling of absolute tyrannical power up there on the mound. I remember the grin on my catcher Jerry's face as he called for the curveball. I remember a procession of big, dumb-looking pituitary cases from Lennox, or Westchester, or Azusa, or one of the other interchangeable fast-food suburbs of Los Angeles, coming up to the plate. They looked like they were about to shit in their pants at the prospect of some crazy Jewish kid throwing them a curveball aimed right at their hip bone! After the game, my mom bought me hot dogs because I had done so well. I basked in the glory and made an early connection: athletic achievement leads to mother love.

□

This period of my life also marks the point at which I began to read. My friend Joe used to carry around dog-eared copies of histories of World War II (one of Churchill's series of books or Shirer's *The Rise and Fall of the Third Reich*). I thought he was really cool. I wanted to be cool too so I started reading some novels. I gravitated toward the existentialists, some of the simpler books by Camus, with a little Kafka thrown in on the side. Although much of their meaning eluded my twelve-year-old's level of comprehension, I was enjoying reading and it was expanding my mind. If nothing else, I was improving my vocabulary and developing an alternative to television, which I now consider to be a waste of time and harmful to a developing child's mind.

CHAPTER THREE

High School

Beverly Hills High School stands upon a set of beautifully terraced, rolling hills on the edge of the bountiful tax base that supports it so well. More than well, actually. The school displays meticulously kept tennis courts, an excellent library, and an extraordinary "Little Theatre" that many professional companies would be ecstatic to call their own. Beverly also has a basketball gymnasium that features a floor that separates in the center and electronically slides apart to reveal an Olympic-sized swimming pool. During my time there, oil was discovered on campus. This didn't hurt the already robust fiscal picture of the school. If anyone comes knocking on your door to collect donations for Beverly Hills High, don't give them anything.

The four elementary schools of Beverly Hills all funnel their children into Beverly Hills High. The high school becomes a place where one can meet and mix with the other wealthy youngsters against whom you have played intramural sports. For me, however, there wasn't much of this intermingling. I retained my elementary school buddies all through high school. I was intimidated by the move from the cozy familiarity of my elementary school to the more foreign hustle and bustle of Beverly. Everyone else seemed so at home, so popular, and so happy.

I began to feel terribly self-conscious. I still didn't know what the hell to do about girls. I felt awful about my looks. I hated my curly hair. I now love to hear that people are paying money to get the permanent wave that I have naturally. I began to wonder about my identity. Everyone else appeared to have one. Where was mine? I was a late bloomer in an environment of achievement-oriented kids. How could I know then that I would be twenty-three before I would choose a career? That I would be twenty-five before I was confident sexually or socially? And what's wrong with any of that? It would have been comforting then to have heard a wise voice in my ear saying, *Don't get too worried. You'll find yourself. People usually do. Just relax and enjoy the ride 'cause it's gonna be bumpy!* But the voice never materialized. During this period I was facing the initial confrontation with the abyss of my identity. I was losing my false sense of being in control of the world. I was becoming aware that life is considerably more complex and challenging than simply throwing strikes in a baseball game.

In the four years I served with honor and distinction at Beverly, I ate lunch at school less than ten times. When the lunch bell rang I would hustle home for a quick bite to eat. By not eating on the school's front lawn with my peers, I avoided potentially threatening contact with them. Looking back, it's difficult for me to believe that

I was running so scared. I've lived with imminent death staring at me for two years now and I've learned not to be afraid of that. People don't make me insecure anymore. There is no judgment, criticism, or attitude anyone can hold that would frighten me.

During these high school days, many of my fears centered on the female segment of society. I had crazy, fantastic, (unconscious?) illusions about them. I felt that I had to treat them differently from males. I now believe that the major distinctions between women and men stem from the conditioning inherent in our patriarchal society. During these youthful days I could only discern the differences, not the reasons why. I had no idea where these differences came from or what to do about the fact that they existed. I didn't know how to begin relating to girls. My sex drive was starting to coalesce into the adolescent obsession that is considered normal for young boys in our society. I didn't have a clue about how to deal with it. I could sense my powerful, angry, neurotic iceberg of a sex drive and I was intuitively afraid.

My freshman year was noteworthy in that I received straight As and I participated on the forensic team as a debater. My partner was none other than my steadfast friend Joe.

The topic for debate that year was: "Resolved: That the United States should immediately suspend the draft and switch to an all-volunteer army." Joe and I went to the library to do our initial research the day before our first debate. We wrote up over fifty note cards filled with relevant data and quotations about the subject at hand. Courageously, we entered our first debate with the note cards neatly filed in a small 3 x 5-inch box. We were stunned to see our opponents enter the room accompanied by a stand-up filing cabinet filled with note cards mounted on a refrigerator dolly.

Each of the other two teams we faced that day had been equally fanatical in the thoroughness of their research. Needless to say, we were soundly trounced in rounds one, two, and three. These lunatics from the other schools were playing hardball while we had prepared for a game of badminton.

Joe and I conferred about our situation prior to the next scheduled debate. We concluded that there was no way we could out-research these maniacs. Our rivals obviously had nothing better to do with their empty evenings and weekends than hang around library research stacks gathering irrefutable quotes and data about the efficacy of the all-volunteer army. We knew we would get burned if we tried to do it their way, so we hit on a plan of our own. We showed up at the next debate with our meager supply of index cards, in addition to a healthy reserve of blanks. We knew that every major contention of the enemy team could be refuted with a little imagination and a sliding scale of morality. It worked like a charm!

Our opponents' jaws dropped as we produced index cards filled with recantations of their major quotations, not to mention superior, updated data that completely destroyed their most important contentions. They looked in awe at our tiny box of index cards, trying to figure out how we had managed to choose the appropriate one hundred out of the thousands of cards we undoubtedly had left at home. Little did they realize that we were furiously scribbling down the cards as the debate progressed, and that our quotations were mere products of our fertile and amoral imaginations. We thoroughly destroyed our first set of opponents. Following the debate, they approached us deferentially to offer their congratulations. We thrashed our next two sets of opponents to win gold medals. For the rest of the year we went undefeated.

Each debate was observed by a referee who determined the winners. The only judge who worried us was the notorious "Clock Judge." Debates were limited by time. Most of the judges were content to rely upon the school clocks in the classrooms to give an accurate measure of time. Not the Clock Judge. This crazy dude actually carried around an egg timer, which would start to ring annoyingly when a debater's time was up. The Clock Judge loved his tiny toy, fondling it, winding it, and playing with it at every opportunity.

By a twist of fate, we drew the Clock Judge as our referee an inordinate number of times. He started to get suspicious after he saw us unmercifully flogging our opponents in every debate, using only our bogus box of index cards. We tried to ease his obvious suspicion by bringing in progressively larger and more impressive filing cabinets, but I'm sure the Clock Judge smelled a rat. He never said anything to us directly, but at times I would make contact with his beady little black eyes and I'd sense the spinning of his gears. I knew the Clock Judge was thinking, "Boy, I don't know what your game is but I know that something fishy is going on, and when I find out what it is, I'm gonna put my foot down on you and squish you like a little bug!"

Fortunately, the Clock Judge never figured out our scam. After that first year together as debate partners, Joe and I retired—to the great dismay of the forensics department. My parents proudly displayed my gold medals in our living room.

□

I know that I studied hard and did quite well academically during my first two years of high school. I remember only one of my teachers from this period. She impressed me more with her sadism than with her ability to teach.

Frau D. taught German. I chose to take this language because I had done so pitifully in elementary school Spanish, and French seemed awfully prissy to me. German is actually a very pleasant language. We

Americans are conditioned by years of hearing Nazis issue guttural commands in World War II movies. It is difficult for us to get beyond our appropriate hatred of Nazism and appreciate that German is pleasing to the ear. The language offers the student the advantage of reflecting a typically Germanic need for order. Its syntax follows quite regular rules and there are very few exceptions.

Frau D. was a tight-lipped lady of Italian descent. She was fond of saying things like, "Kinder, do not speak to me of eating corn! Corn iz not for humans to eat. Corn iz fur barnyard animals to fatten zem up!"

I was sure she had been a Fascist during the war and I hated her with a passion. Sometimes Frau D. would slip and say things that indicated her political sympathies. One day a student walked innocently into class with a baseball cap on his head. He sat down without removing the cap. Frau D. began to shake visibly. "Herr S., take off zat kap! Zis iz a skool-room, not a synagogue!"

All of Frau D.'s students detested her. Cheating and misbehavior became rampant in her class. There were not many students interested in taking German. This was attributable to both the growing reputation of Frau D.'s gestapo mentality and the fact that 98 percent of the kids at Beverly were Jewish. There was a two-year minimum requirement of a single language in order to graduate, so once a student had survived a semester or two of Frau D., he or she had a lot of incentive to keep on going. As a result, our class had a small but stable enrollment from semester to semester.

Frau D. began to sense that she was losing control of us during my sophomore year. She instituted a new and completely idiosyncratic policy of daily trips to the "language laboratory." This bizarre and useless place no doubt owed its existence to one of LBJ's Great Society educational programs. These policies ended up paying companies like Westinghouse lots of money to design, build, and implement largely ineffective "teaching machines." These gadgets did nothing to benefit the hordes of unlucky students who were forced to use them.

Malcolm X was functionally illiterate until he was imprisoned in his twenties. At this point in his life, with the aid of a dictionary and a Bible, he taught himself how to read—alone in a jail cell. I was once picked up hitchhiking by a university professor of sociology. He had yanked his daughter out of high school because he was afraid that her brain "was turning into mush." Since leaving school, she spent her days successfully marketing the stained-glass products that she was so good at making. She was also plowing through the Durants' *The Story of Civilization*, which she discussed with her father in the evenings.

I cite these examples to illustrate that the problems within the educational system today are unrelated to our "educational technology." A motivated seventeen-year-old can pick up everything I learned from four years of high school in six months of focused study. Technological advances such as the language lab don't even begin to address the basic problem: student motivation.

When I was in high school I saw mathematics as being totally irrelevant to my life. As a result, I had trouble comprehending the simplest algebraic equation. When I returned to college to study science, I quickly realized that I would never understand certain concepts of biology without some basic comprehension of physics. Understanding physics, in turn, depended on a working knowledge of calculus. It was only then that math became relevant and understandable.

The problem today is that the high school curriculum appears totally irrelevant to the captive student. I discovered on my own that I enjoyed reading and had a thirst for knowledge. I don't know where this thirst comes from, but I suspect that it represents the intersection of both cultural and familial values. I don't sense this thirst in most kids I meet. The ones who have it are quite refreshing.

☐

I recently gave a lecture to a class of high school juniors on the workings of the human circulatory system. I must confess that I was shocked at their total lack of interest in the material I had so carefully prepared. My first reaction was one of anger. Why weren't these little people paying

attention? Right in the middle of my talk it hit me, *Hey,
I didn't give a damn about any of this when I was seventeen
years old... why should they?*

Attempts at making a curriculum that is more "relevant" are usually misguided and end up disappointing the
student. I think that high school attendance should be
voluntary. Kids this age should be learning how to make
decisions and the most important decision they can make
is how to utilize their youth. I believe that kids should
only attend the classes of their choice. As a result, high
schools would have a highly committed body of students
who are learning to make decisions about what they want
to do on their own. Also, I would not have college accep-
tance in any way contingent upon high school performance. Colleges should have a place for those who didn't
attend high school because they opted to try real life for
a while.

Unfortunately for her students, Frau D. did not share
my laissez-faire view of schoolroom politics. We were her
(Jewish) captives and she was determined to teach us the
mysteries of the German language, even (especially) if the
process killed us.

Frau D. had one overriding obsession: we had to
learn German. I began to see her compulsion in terms of
a larger desire on the part of society, as represented by the
high school, to produce a group of well-rounded generalists. Everybody, no matter what their interests, motivation, or predisposition, had to learn some math, had to

learn some history, had to take "X" hours of "Y" subjects to fulfill our state-mandated program. For many young people a broad exposure to a variety of subjects and experiences is undoubtedly a good idea. Some kids, however, are better off left alone with a chessboard and a key to the school library. High school forces these kids to waste time learning things they will never use. High schools are turning out generalists in a world crying out for specialists.

Frau D.'s undoing came suddenly. One day, one of her spiked heels collapsed and she tripped and fell right in front of the class. There were a few repressed giggles and then an awful silence. No one rose from their chair to help her. Frau D. had broken her ankle and wouldn't be teaching the German class at Beverly Hills High the rest of the year.

CHAPTER FOUR

High School Revisited

In my third year of high school I went out for baseball and made the junior varsity team as a pitcher. I hadn't played baseball in the three years since Little League, and it was a pleasant surprise to find that my fastball still had a little zip on it at a major league pitching distance. It was a good feeling to be back out on a baseball diamond. Being selected for the team provided enough ego gratification to bring my disquieting "Search for Identity" to a temporary halt.

My first game was against a Catholic boys' school. I was scheduled to pitch innings four, five, and six. Our starting pitcher got into trouble in the first inning so I was put in the game early. When I entered there were two men out, the bases were loaded, and the other team had already scored four runs. Mr. M. was the coach of my team. He was a former army drill sergeant who maintained his DI mentality and flattop crew cut during his tenure as JV baseball coach. Coach M. was out on the mound waiting for me. He was ready to hand over the ball and give me some sage advice.

"Now, Jimmy!" he barked. "I don't want you messin' around tryin' to strike everybody out! Jes' you concentrate on throwin' strikes and let the guys behind you do all the work."

Alright, I thought to myself, I'll just try and let these guys hit the ball. The first guy comes up and I throw the ball in there nice and low and straight. The batter hits an easy one on the ground to my second baseman, who proceeds to let the ball go right between his legs. Now we're losing by six runs. The next guy comes up and I throw some pitches right down the pike and eventually he hits a soft one to shallow right field. My right fielder collides with my first baseman. My first baseman drops the ball as a result, and now we're down by seven runs. There's still two men on base and Coach M. comes to the mound again for a little pep talk.

"Hey, Jimmy, don't you worry son, yer doin' a heck of a good job. If you had any kinda team behind you out here you'd be in good shape...so jes' keep on chuckin'."

So the next guy walks up to the plate and I'm saying to myself, "Screw this! The only way that I'm getting out of this mess is to strike the next dude out!" Let's face it, this situation was getting desperate and these clowns out here on the field were only going to make things worse. I made a quick decision to revert to my Little League strategy which had been so successful many years ago. The old curveball would have to do the trick.

I remember the next pitch as clearly as I recollect my first sexual experience. I visualize everything in super-slow motion. There is fear in the batter's eyes as he sees my pitch heading right for his hip bone. He experiences a moment of pure terror and total indecision, a millisecond or two when his central nervous system turns into lime Jell-O. His reflexes freeze, and he thinks to himself, "Please God, don't let that ball hit me, please God, oh God, no God, I'm too young to die!!!" Then his baseball instincts take over and he bends neatly out of the way just in time to watch the ball take a sharp left-hand turn as it falls off the edge of an imaginary table, right in there for "Steeeerike Three! Batter, you are OUTTATHERE!!!"

The next inning I did the same thing. I threw as hard as I could on every pitch until I had two strikes on the batter—then I would break off a nasty little curveball. I struck out three more men in a row after my first victim. Only the last batter I faced even bothered to swing at strike three. The swing was a weak effort on his part, which produced nothing but air.

The intense pain in my right arm that evening should have been warning enough for me to take care of myself, but I didn't. I threw too hard, and I continued to throw too many curveballs. I put too much stress on my developing adolescent shoulder. Many years later, a professor in an anatomy class would tell me that I had caused a stretching of the tendon of the long head of the biceps, and that I should have rested my arm completely for at least a month upon first noticing the pain. Instead, I continued to pitch. I was constantly asked to throw batting practice because I was the only pitcher on our team with any control. Being such a good batting practice pitcher meant that I was throwing the ball hard on my regular days off. Over the next couple of months my arm started to hurt so badly that I couldn't raise it to answer a question in class. I pitched pretty well for the first five weeks of the season but then my arm completely gave out. I had absolutely nothing left on my fastball, and was forced to endure some rather brutal shellings.

I should have developed my arm properly. I should have continued to play organized ball after Little League. I should have said something to the coach when my arm began to hurt, but I was all caught up in the "bite the bullet" propaganda of high school athletics: "Triumph is just 'try' with a little 'umph' added to it. When the going gets tough, the tough get going." I should have gone up to Coach M. and said, "You know, Coach . . . I don't want to let the team down but my arm feels like it's been run over by a tractor, and maybe I should lay off throwing for a while." Had I done this he would have looked at me as if I was a Communist sympathizer or a homosexual. In the long run, however, my persistence in ruining my arm was a good thing. I was forced to leave my baseball days behind and go on to more enlightening pursuits, such as getting stoned, growing my hair, and listening to music.

These activities became the major foci of my energies in the year following my JV baseball debacle. One day at school my friend Bobby and I got identical notes during class saying that the varsity baseball coach wanted to see us in his office later that afternoon. Bobby, had been a starting pitcher on the junior varsity team with me. We realized that the coach was going to push us to try out again in the spring. We knew that the upcoming meeting was likely to be uncomfortable, so we smoked some dope out in Bobby's car to prepare. By the time of our appointment we were both thoroughly wasted.

Coach F. was sitting behind his desk in the athletic department. He was gripping and ungripping a hard rubber ball the entire time he spoke to us, using his big meaty hands, first the right for a while, and then a shift to the left, back to the right, left, right, on and on, over and over, again and again, endlessly. These were the same hands that had played All-League catcher for Beverly Hills High not many years ago; the same hands that patted us on our rear ends when we made a good play; and the same hands that would soon be convicted of child molestation. He waved one of his beefy paws to indicate that we should sit down. I was very stoned. I was intently attending to my every move with the paranoia induced by being high. I couldn't help being distracted by the two little drops of sweat on Coach F.'s upper lip as he droned on and on about the importance of the baseball program at Beverly Hills High. He assured us that we would look back on these years with a special fondness for our sacrifice to the team effort. By this time the coach was really rolling but I had stopped listening. I was concentrating on the sweat beads and I was wondering how long they had been perched on the ledge of the coach's upper lip. Suddenly I realized that the coach had stopped short and delivered the punch line.

"Fellas...Do you know who I think I'm looking at right now?"

Well, he was obviously staring at us.

"I think that I just might be looking at two members of the starting rotation of next year's varsity club." At this point Coach F. threw in a lengthy pause.

I guess it was the long silence that did it. I looked over at Bobby and all I could see was a long-haired pothead whose brain presently had the consistency of a poached egg. At the same time he looked over at me and must have seen someone who more closely resembled Rasputin the Mad Monk than a high school baseball player. We caught each other's eyes for a split second, and that did us in. We started giggling. The giggling led to the snorting sound that comes from trying to restrain laughter. Finally there was great, uncontrolled screaming, wailing, tearful laughter. Coach F. had the look of a man who had accidentally parachuted onto another planet, but he nervously joined in the laughter as if he understood the joke. As we left the office I could see him going through the mental gyrations of excluding us from next year's plans.

□

My best experience of high school was my involvement in the drama department as a member of the stage crew. One of the great things about my high school was the number of different avenues open to the student for the achievement of peer respect. One didn't have to be a jock or a stoner to make friends at Beverly Hills High. I wasted two years trying to prove myself as an athlete (which I certainly was not!). I then went out for stage crew on a whim because my friend Joe was a hotshot actor. I had a fantastic time working on the school plays and derived many benefits from the experience.

Not the least important benefit was meeting up with my first sweetheart, K.T. She was in one of the school plays that I worked on. At the cast party after the last performance, K.T. and I talked for hours. I went home and carefully evaluated every word she had said. I decided that I would ask her to go out. It took me a week to get up the courage to make the call. I dialed the first six digits of her phone number a thousand times before finally making the connection. On our first date we went to Hollywood to see Vincent Price star in the 3D version of *House of Wax*. During the movie I put my arm around her, and when she didn't resist, I kissed her on the lips. We left the theater twenty minutes into the feature and went across the street to a coffee shop. K.T. had tea and some kind of cream pie. I forget what I ate.

K.T. was a wonderful young woman. She was cute, small, smart, and warm. She liked music, was very gentle with me, and was intellectually precocious. I had a fantastic time with her. We were both sexually ignorant and our relationship became a good learning experience for each of us. After an initial month of intense kissing, she told me that I could "go farther if I wanted." Well, I wanted, and one thing led to another and pretty soon we were going to bed together completely nude. K.T. decided she would take birth control pills so that we could begin to have intercourse.

Well, my big opportunity had arrived! I was finally going to be de-virginized! K.T. and I attended a Planned Parenthood lecture. We were the most naïve couple there. Our counselor took extra time with us. I didn't know a condom from a camshaft. I needed all the information I could get.

My first two stabs at intercourse were notably unsuccessful. Finally being able to have sex made me nervous. My raging adolescent sex drive turned to mush, and my penis, which had been permanently erect for the past six years, suddenly became as limp as yesterday's spaghetti.

I became despondent. I remember writing my friend Joe a note during English class. It began, "Dear Joe, There's something I've got to tell you. You have don't have to hang around with me anymore because I think I'm gay." Joe assured me, later, that I was just nervous. He was more experienced sexually than I was, and I took new hope from his diagnosis.

The third try worked out well. As a matter of fact, it was terrific. I went over to K.T.'s house one morning after her parents had left for work. She answered the door, wearing her cute little nightgown with the hole in the sleeve. She had just gotten out of bed and was still sleepy-eyed and relaxed. I still remember the warmth of her body as we made love. Afterward, we took a long nap. I woke up to the afternoon sun streaming through the yellow curtains of K.T.'s little girl room, giving the room a warm, bright glow. I was very happy, and evidently, so was K.T. We continued our sexual experiments on floors, in cars, at friend's houses, in the bushes at UCLA, on camping trips, in the park, whenever and wherever we could. We both enjoyed the opportunity to explore the wide expanses of sexuality with a relaxed partner. I know that she was great for me, and I felt like a normal guy for the first time in years.

My last few months of high school were good times in my life. They were filled with K.T., hitchhiking, friends, music, getting high, playing guitar, staying up late, and working on the stage crew at school. The theater arts teachers liked my work, and I was given the responsibilities of stage manager for the department's production of *Our Town*. I promptly responded to their confidence in me by screwing up the play's last act. My only duty in this act was to set up three rows of chairs for the big finale—the graveyard scene. For some reason I neglected to set up one row of chairs. I wasn't even stoned or drunk. I just forgot.

Baseball, girls, my first job, cars, curly hair, friends, stage crew, classes, homework, poker games, getting high, playing guitar, listening to music, Kerouac, getting in trouble, hitchhiking, the beach, insecurities appearing like little pimples, the Beatles and the Rolling Stones, the war in Vietnam, walking to school, getting stoned in the park, coaching Little League, beating up my brother, putting down my sister, Chinese food with my parents, birthdays, good days, bad days, clear days, football days, TV days, K.T. days, all those days, and now they're gone. What did they all mean? I can't add them up or keep them in reserve to fall back on. Nobody will allow me to use them as collateral, or to relive them, or to understand them. They are like a giant piece of film with each day represented by a single frame. They've been run through my projector, but now everything is messed up by my tumor and I'm stuck on the superfast speed. The damn thing is going too fast. Somebody better shut me down. Isn't there a doctor in the house who can help?

CHAPTER FIVE

Hitchhiking

THE DAY THAT HIGH SCHOOL ENDED JOE AND I ate some peyote. Carlos Castaneda's books had impressed us deeply. In his stories, Castaneda describes a wonderful series of adventures he had while taking peyote under the tutelage of a Mexican holy man. I had a marvelous reaction to the drug—nausea, vomiting, and an acute anxiety attack. I reached the peak of this whole experience when I blew my groceries in a friend's bathroom. I was having visual hallucinations about the hole at the bottom of the toilet. Joe prevented me from climbing into the bowl. The evening left me with the profound realization that I had no direction in my life.

The next morning, Joe and I picked a direction—due north—and we were off on our hitchhiking trip. Our plan wasn't much of a plan at all. We each had a few hundred bucks, two months to kill until college began, and a vague desire to send postcards home from the Big Apple. We didn't know where we were going to eat or sleep. We had no idea of how long the next ride might be or with whom it might be, or whether there would even be another ride. I guess that was the point of the whole thing. Not knowing or planning anything gave us

a powerful feeling of freedom. We were limited to the
options that were offered to us by the road. These always
turned out to be enough for our needs, and sometimes
even plentiful. We learned that it doesn't take living in
Beverly Hills to be happy. We also saw that it doesn't take
a Porsche to make it across the country. In fact, it doesn't
take much at all if you're willing to hitchhike. Just a little
patience and a little luck. Patience and luck and a func-
tional right thumb. That's all you need.

The first thing that we had to do was get the peyote out of our brains. Joe's cerebrum was still perco-
lating during our first night's stay at a public park in
Sacramento, "Sacto," California. He had handled the
initial onslaught of the drug much better than I, but
he was now seeing lots of "pictures" in the sky. We were
starting an unnerving number of identical sentences
simultaneously. I was often startled to hear Joe giving
voice to my thoughts. A good night's sleep and some
hot coffee brought us both a little closer to sea level. We
were off!

Redding, the last city of any consequence in California, passed by in a flash. Route 5 took us right through
the top of the state and into the lovely land of Oregon,
or "Oregun" as many Californians pronounce it. We were
out of our home state! Oregon is a wonderful world pop-
ulated with friendly people, incredible scenery, a good
Shakespeare festival in Ashland, and policemen who stop
hitchhikers on sight ... to make sure they're all right! "All

right? Why, Mr. Policeman, we're doing just fine and dandy! You aren't gonna bust us? Hey, how do we become citizens of this strange land?"

□

Oregon offered up some beautiful camping in the Rogue River Valley and in Ainsworth State Park, just outside of Portland. A crazy old geezer with a VA hospital wristband tried to drive off with our stuff. Joe saved the day by hanging onto the car door as the lunatic pulled away. I guess the guy was in touch enough with reality to want to avoid a murder rap, so he stopped. Joe got to keep his life, and we both got our clothes back. We left Oregon to escape the ever present rains. Idaho, another beautiful state, loomed ahead. In Boise we received our first lesson in "home state food specialties": Don't eat them. Our Boise breakfast included some of the poorest excuses for home fries that I had ever tasted. Wait a second—wasn't this Idaho, home of the potato, land of spuds? What gives here? After a number of similar experiences, Joe and I would come to the conclusion that most home state food specialties are exported. This creates a favorable balance of trade, but unfortunately leaves the home state market shelves bare. Try to find a good potato in Idaho or a decent steak in Omaha....

It's difficult to convey the sense of cultural disorientation that we felt during our stay in Wyoming. The first tip-off that this was going to be a bizarre place came during our initial gas stops. Every gas station was set up identically, with the same little coffee shops and the same gas coming out of the same pumps, always arranged the same way. It was as though we had landed in the People's Republic of Wyoming!

Outside of this stab at nationalization and centralized control, nothing in Wyoming was very remarkable. Well, that's not entirely true. The desert in this part of the country is incredibly beautiful in a subtle way. The more I looked out at the desert passing by, the more I could discern the shadings of purples and lavenders and reds. It's strange, but it takes a concerted effort to make out all of these shades. It's similar to staring at the night sky—the longer you look, the more stars you see.

After just fourteen hours in Wyoming, Joe and I left Cheyenne via Greyhound bus. While Joe made time with a girl he met on the Hound, I looked out the window at the country passing by. Gas stations, freeways, farms, billboards, junked car bodies, restaurants, Dairy Queens—this was my damn country! Inside I felt a struggle going on between a disquieting alienation from what was outside the window and some kind of instinctive love for what I saw. It was the same type of love I had for my parents. I didn't always like the way they were. I didn't understand why they were the way they were. But they were my parents, and I loved them. This was my society, my country. I was disconnected from it, but looking through the bus window made me realize that it was a part of me, and I loved it.

Joe's girl lived in North Platte, Nebraska. We ended up sleeping in a field on the outskirts of town. Mosquitoes feasted on us throughout the night. The next day, a lonely old alcoholic guy with a wooden leg took us into Joliet, Illinois. It was raining hard when we arrived. He put us up for the night on his floor.

Chicago, "Chitown," "The Windy City," was our next stop. We had a good time there. We checked out the Cubbies at Wrigley Field, the Chicago cops on State Street, and some funky Jewish soul food from Joe's grandma. We hitchhiked out of town from a freeway entrance on the South Side. This is a large, black ghetto, famous for its brand of electric blues music. Joe is now a resident of Chicago and he informs me that choosing this area as our point of departure was about as smart as taking a bike ride in the countryside surrounding Da Nang in the middle of the Tet Offensive. Somehow we survived.

A series of rides took us to Yellow Springs, Ohio, so we could visit Antioch College, my high school sweetie's new home. K.T. had started school early in the summer and by the time I hit town she was well into her new groove: new friends, new boys, and new ideas about old relationships. Antioch was a unique school. The pupils and professors were basically indistinguishable. There was the smell of educational freedom in the classrooms. There was the smell of high quality pot in the dorms. I chose to take advantage of the latter.

After a while, the place started to get to me. The summer heat in Yellow Springs was almost unbearable. K.T. hinted that there was a new mule kicking in my stall, and Joe was involved in an affair of the heart that was going nowhere at a moderately fast speed. We decided to hit the road again. That was the beauty of this trip. We could always keep on moving.

□

Hitchhiking in the East proved to be a piece of cake in comparison to our experiences in Wyoming. It was so easy that I don't remember most of the rides. I do know that we made it safely, and quickly to Washington, DC. And it was all for free! Hitchhiking was such a simple game to play. All we had to do was stick out a thumb, and wait . . . limmmmmmummimmmumummmmaimmalmmwhoooooooooooooooooshhmmmmmmmmmmmmmmmmmmwhooooooooo ooooooooooooooooooooooooooossssssssssshhhhhhhhhhmmmmmmmmmmmmmmmmmmmmmm mmmmmmmmwhooooooooooooooooshhhhhhhhhhhhh.

"Did you see that last guy? He could've stopped—he had plenty of room!"

(Five minutes without a car.) "This is a slow spot. Hey Joe, what's today, Sunday? I'm starting to forget what month it is. Time to whip out the old Hohner Marine Band harmonica in the blues key of F. 'I'm goin' down to the crossroads mama, believe I'll flag a...'

"Hhhhhhhmmmmmwhoooooooooooooooooooooooooooooooshhhhhhhhhhhh.

"Shit. That guy coulda stopped....nobody is stoppin." 'My best friends done passed me by.' Here it comes, here it comes, is this guy pullin' over or what? I wanna make my move, yeah, buddy all right! Come and get us mister, take us outta here, this place is the pits."

"Hi! Where you headed?"

"We're tryin' to make it to New York City."

"Oh...No."

"That's all right. Thanks anyway. Thanks a lot for stopping!" 'I'm goin' down to the crossroads, take my rider by my side...'

Eventually we landed in New York, "The Big Apple," "Gotham," "The City." I immediately bought a thirty-cent Italian ice for a dollar. The street vendor just took my buck and moved on. I wasn't aggressively hostile enough for this place. Joe and I both loved The City. It certainly deserves its nickname. New York offers up all of the standard big-city fare, but it has everything ten times larger, brighter, and more expensive than anywhere else. It offered us two young women whom Joe met in Central Park. They liked him enough to give him their address in

Tom's River, New Jersey. Tom's River was a stone's throw south of New York—and after two hours of hitchhiking we were there.

Tom's River is a totally nondescript town in the state of New Jersey. Tract houses, mobile homes, Fords, Chevys, Motel 6s, 7-Elevens, industrial smog, polyester clothes, Main Street—Suburbia, U.S.A. We felt as if we had stepped right into a Diane Arbus photograph. We saw a small-town circus and we hung out with our gals. We hit the beaches and saw a movie in town. We were refused service at a restaurant. One night, a local maniac rousted us from the construction site where we were sleeping—at gunpoint! We left pretty soon after that. And went on to better places, more beautiful places.

New England in the late summer is a gorgeous part of the country. Boston, "Beantown," "The Hub," treated us well. Our stay there was filled to the brim with great roast beef sandwiches, wonderful walks on the Common, visits to historical graveyards, Cambridge bookstores, old friends, and warm get-togethers with aunts and uncles. A trip to Vermont and New Hampshire allowed us to visit the small private colleges that we would be attending in September. These were sobering days, filled with the realization that we would soon be locked up in these places for good. It dawned on us that we had almost used up our summer vacation: six of the nine weeks were gone. The whole thing had passed so quickly! It seemed like one beat of our hearts since we had left home. The freedom of the road and the constancy of our motion had made time fly. Hey, wait a minute. We just started this trip. Weren't we in Sacto a couple of days ago . . . SIX WEEKS?

□

We decided to hightail it back across the country in order to leave as much time as possible for California. We had been in too much of a hurry to give our own home state the proper respect. The ride home was a wild flight of around-the-clock hitching. We were able to flag down rides with amazing ease. I remember lying to a guy about being able to handle the stick shift of his foreign car. He woke up from a nap just in time to see me almost kill us all in a desperate attempt to stop for gas. He drove the rest of the way.

There was a short visit to my birthplace, Buffalo, New York. We saw Niagara Falls, and our driver managed to get two moving violations within a half hour. Buffalo is a desperately depressing place. It neither has, nor deserves a nickname. We got a memorable ride from a trucker who picked us up just outside of Philadelphia, "Philly," "The City of Brotherly Love." He had performed sexual intercourse with "every barnyard animal 'cept a guinea hen, and I woulda tried one if they weren't so goddam small!" There was another ride with a serviceman from Wisconsin who confessed to sleeping with his sister: "Now I'm not defending myself, but when that snow starts coming down every winter and you're stuck out on that farm together, your sister starts to look pretty good..."

There were wide open plains, wheat fields, cotton fields, and corn fields stretching out as far as the eye could see—an ocean of corn. There were farms, houses, churches, highways, byways, state roads, bridges, dams, lakes, rivers, big towns, small towns, hamlets, villages, big cities, little cities, state capitals, speed traps, cows, state police, meadows, fences, cheap gas, oil fields, state parks, truck stops, off-roads, shortcuts, overpasses, on-ramps, off-ramps, sunsets, night drives, speed bumps, hot cars, big cars, small cars, fast cars, slow cars, loud cars, and people, all the crazy people who gave us rides.

Joe and I had a running philosophical discussion about these people, about the citizens of our huge land. Were they basically good or bad? Would people withstand the scrutiny of our moral microscope? Weren't we acting as living litmus paper, testing the acidity of every person who passed us with room to spare, a full tank, and lots of miles ahead? Each of us would successfully argue both sides of the issue, depending on how we felt at any given moment. Both positions were easily justifiable. On the one hand, 99.9 percent of the drivers passed us by. People are shmucks! Then somebody would stop, give us a lift, treat us to a meal, and put us up for a night. People could be so kind! I now believe that people are neither good nor bad in any absolute sense. Rather, they have a range of potentialities, a host of possible behaviors—all waiting to be expressed. Environment, culture, social forces: these determine which behaviors will rise to the surface.

Joe and I hitchhiked day and night on our whirlwind tour back across the country. We were running low on time but we managed to score several long distance rides. Missouri, "Missou," Kansas, we're in the Corn Belt, Nebraska, the "Cornhusker State," Oklahoma, "O.K.," New Mexico, "Land of the Midnight Sun," and then Colorado, our downfall state. Colorado has tight prohibitions against hitchhiking. Coloradans are more than willing to put hitchhikers in jail for thirty days. Just as we did in Wyoming, we decided to remove our bodies from this place by the quickest means possible, the Greyhound bus.

We hopped the Hound to Salt Lake City, Utah. Joe and I felt sorry for an alcoholic bum who spare-changed us as we got off the bus. We figured the guy probably didn't eat well, so we bought him a dinner. We heaped his plate full of fried chicken, mashed potatoes with gravy, and vegetables. The old codger took one spoonful of lima beans and proceeded to fall into an alcoholic stupor. His head plopped right into the mashed potatoes. The dark-brown gravy complemented his graying hair nicely. We left him alone to sleep. Salt Lake City turned out to be the cleanest, and dullest big city in the United States. We felt dirty and bored there. We thumbed our way quickly through Utah and Nevada. Pretty soon, we were back in our home state of California. The trip from New Hampshire had taken less than five days.

California, the "Golden State," land of milk and honey. The country is tipped and all of the nuts roll out here! Oh, paradise on earth, our poor neglected home state. Here we had gone and hitchhiked 7,000 miles and there was so much waiting for us in California. It was nice to be home.

For a start, there was San Francisco, "Frisco," "San Fran," "The City." (Well, New Yorkers might give you an argument over that last one. New Yorkers will give you an argument over anything.) Across the bay was Berkeley, "Bezerkley," land of the street people, where leftist politics, dope, and counterculture abounded. Joe and I took advantage of the youthful spirit there. He had an affair with a woman he met, and I went to an excellent Grateful Dead concert.

We headed south on State Route 1 for our stretch run home. This state highway is one of the most beautiful roads in the world. YOUR HONOR, I OBJECT. The writer has not seen all of the world and cannot possibly know which roads are more or less beautiful. OVERRULED. The statement will stand. Well, let's put it this way: it's hard to imagine a more beautiful road. Heading south on Route 1 from San Francisco to Los Angeles affords a breathtaking view of the Pacific Ocean on the right, and the spectacular California redwoods on the left. There are also many Californians hitchhiking on both sides of the road. The competition made this relatively short stretch slow going.

By the time we got home to Los Angeles, "L.A.," "City of Angels," we were both on edge. We took a city bus home from the beach. Joe and I had our first argument on this, the last day of our trip. Although I forget what it was about, I know it was a real barn burner. Joe got off the bus first. We were no longer on speaking terms. We grunted our barely civil goodbyes.

On the bus ride to my house, I had plenty of time to think. I realized that Joe and I weren't really pissed off at each other. We were angry that the trip was over. No more going nowhere, no more circular motion. We had to hop the Eastern College Express Line, the straight track, tried and true. We had parents to please, expectations to fulfill. Joe was on his way to Dartmouth College, a bona-fide Ivy League School, Nelson Rockefeller's alma mater, go Big Green. I was headed for Middlebury College in Vermont, the oldest private coeducational college in the U. S. of A. Go Panthers!

Well, that's where I was going, and not via hitchhiking. Instead, I would take a big jet plane with predetermined times of departure and arrival, a movie, a meal, plenty of bathrooms, and an expensive price tag. For the amount of money my parents shelled out for that five-hour plane ride, I could've lived comfortably on the road for two months. But I wasn't raised to be a bum. I had a future to invest in. I was goal oriented. Going somewhere might yield something that going nowhere had not. After all, the road would always be out there beckoning. I could always return.

CHAPTER SIX

Jobs, Socialism, and the Collected Wisdom of R. L. Jones

I SPENT THE FIVE YEARS AFTER HIGH SCHOOL ON a wild goose chase, running doggedly in search of my "identity." I wasn't even sure that it existed. Every time I'd track it down somewhere it had just cleared out of town, taking the pretty girl and the new car, and leaving the mortgage payments behind for me to handle. Where was my identity hiding, how many years would it take to find it, how far behind everyone else would I be when I finally did?

I kept looking for my calling, something out there with JIM SLOTNICK etched on it, something permanent that I could enjoy and that would shield me from pain. Subconsciously, I defined life as suffering and I glorified my neuroses by changing them into fragments of the "existential dilemma." From existentialism to socialism by way of alcoholism, cold women, crummy low-paying jobs and trouble, trouble, trouble, right here in River City! I should have borrowed a page from Mao centralized and developed a five-year plan. I needed a blueprint designed to get me on the right track to somewhere, anywhere! Instead of following a plan, my life went zig-zagging along, lurching and sliding irregularly. Sometimes there was too much alcohol, for a while there was too much dope, and there was usually an extreme shortage of nice women. Centralized control, a planned economy, that's what I needed! I had nothing to lose but my neuroses, my psychological chains! First-born Jewish males of the world, UNITE!

□

I've been a pirate, a poet
a puppet, a pauper
a pawn, a king
I've been up and down and all around
And I know one thing
Each time I fall
Flat on my face
I just pick myself up
And get back in the race
That's life.
　　—from *That's Life*

I've worked as an ice cream scooper, newspaper delivery boy, janitor, Little League umpire, morgue assistant, pathology lab assistant, social service aide for autistic children, liquor clerk, stockboy, carpet salesman (door to door), library clerk, short order cook, sanitation engineer, dishwasher, waiter, freelance motion picture cameraman, assistant cameraman, film editor, assistant editor, assistant soundman, camera department rental manager, film department equipment manager, flower delivery boy, laboratory technician, technologist, research assistant, babysitter, and probably a few other things that I don't presently recall.

I hardly have a nickel to my name. I have never spent money on clothes, or cars, or flashy consumer items. I have a twenty-eight dollar cassette player, a hundred dollar ten-speed bicycle, and all of the books that I could ever hope to read. I've never had any spare cash.

Two plus two equals four, and lots of hard work with nothing to show for it eventually equals socialism. I think my eyes were first opened during a unionization battle at one of my jobs. The bosses were kicking our asses with low pay, long hours, displays of favoritism, and vague promises of the riches to come—once the young company got off the ground. The union people didn't seem much better. They were totally out of touch with our shop's special needs. The government, which rears its head in the form of the National Labor Relations Board, sets most of the ground rules. These rules end up helping the bosses by slowing down the whole process.

The certification election took place almost a year after our initial contact with the union. During this period we were carrot-and-sticked to death. Our election ended up in a dead heat and, surprise—it's just like Las Vegas blackjack—the workers lose in a tie! I lost nine months of my life working for peanuts in a hostile environment. The boss thought I was one of the ringleaders of the whole thing (which I was), and he didn't waste too many carrots on me. It was a good experience nonetheless. I learned an important lesson: don't waste time on battles unless you're gonna win!

I followed this axiom closely until I got cancer. When I was first diagnosed as having cancer, I wanted to stop everything so I could have a talk with my tumor. I didn't want to shut down the plant. I wanted to negotiate! I wanted to call time-out and sit down with the damn thing and use a little gentle persuasion. "Listen, you're a tough cookie. I'm not sure I can beat you. I hate to get involved in a losing battle...can't we call the whole thing off?" But that's the problem with cancer. The tumor has all of the control! It sets the stakes at life or death, higher than you care to play. You have no say about where the game is played, any of the ground rules, or the time of play. The damn tumor is your opponent and acts as the referee! No wonder it's so hard to win.

□

My best job ever was when I worked as a short-order cook. Damn, I liked that job. Time flies for a fry cook:

eight hours go by in nothing flat. I rarely had to watch the clock; I was too busy watching the faces of the customers, stocking the garnishes, taking phone orders, and cooking my burgers to worry about time.

Cheeseburgers, hamburgers, french fries, hot dogs, and steak sandwiches: that was the entire bill of fare at Oscar's, corner of Shattuck and Hearst, Berkeley, California—my new home, after transferring to UC Berkeley, following a miserable freshman year at Middlebury. Oscar's was unique in that nothing was written down on checks. All of the orders were placed verbally by the customers of the joint. Patrons waited patiently in line to place their orders directly to the cook. At the lunchtime peak this line would often be fifty people long and stretch halfway down the block. To keep up with the crowd, a fry cook had to handle a grill filled with thirty burgers.

Psychological research indicates that the human brain is only capable of retaining seven (plus or minus one) bits of data at any one time. Well, my first shift as a fry cook certainly bore this out. Any more than two or three orders cooking at one time would overload my circuits. I got so nervous that I was incapable of retaining or cooking much of anything. I soon discovered the secret, however. I had to learn to relax and let my brain take over. I had to learn how not to memorize. I found that as long as I identified a person with his order, as long as I made sure to look at each face as it ordered its meal, then I wouldn't forget. The whole process became automatic. Sometimes my ability to recall an order was quite useful. Imagine being able to approach a woman at a party on Saturday with, "Last Wednesday night you came into Oscar's and ordered a rare cheeseburgerholdthemayoandpickles with fries . . . I don't usually remember customers like this but there was something about you that was so striking, so unique. . . . "

Most self-appointed experts in the art of short-order cuisine judge a cook's expertise solely on the basis of speed. I maintain that it is not speed, but rhythm that is the critical component of this process. I was pretty quick behind the grill, but there were definitely guys who could cook faster. Their edge in speed didn't necessarily make them look as good as me.

It is the rhythm and tempo of the work that makes it beautiful to watch. A good short order cook can be quickly spotted by the internal motion of his work. A polished fry cook will always be moving smoothly. The cerebellum is the key portion of the brain for a short-order cook. I learned in medical school that it is this part of the nervous system that is responsible for smoothing out what would otherwise be jerky motion. My personal experience with damage to my cerebellum from radiation therapy demonstrates that this is true. Cerebellar problems have been the ruin of many a fine short-order cook. A cook with a healthy cerebellum will project a serenity, an exquisite calmness, no matter how many burgers are on the grill. A good cook will be phlegmatic in the face of the most unruly of crowds. After all, the customers will soon be eating happily. All in good time, all in good time.

I became skilled on the grill and soon I could handle the Saturday lunch crowd, the largest of the week. I could have done that job in my sleep. I was cooking up a storm.... I was flying through the place! Turn those three, they're almost ready, get their buns dressed, dip the fries, take another order. Throw on two more, get the fries out of the grease, take three off, and plop, all three patties are on their neatly dressed buns with one fast fry-cook's trick that makes the whole thing look like magic. People love to watch that. Two more burgers, everything on 'em. Next? One burger hold the onions. Next? Next? 'Scuse me, can I help you sir? One steak, medium well, with everything. Dip the fries. Dress some buns. Turn some burgers. Stock the mayo and tomatoes. Hey, Renee, would you grab the phone? Serve up three burgers. Serve up two more with everything. Turn everything left on the grill. Those cooking the longest move to the left. Start some more fries. What a slow day. Where is the lunch crowd? Renee's taking a big phone order. Ten steaks? Are you kidding? How do they want 'em? When do they wanna pick 'em up? Next? We don't have chili. Next? Move the burgers to the left. Move the customers to the left. Head 'em in and head 'em out. Moooo. Just like the cattle that became these burgers. Next? Splat, splat, splat go three cheeseburgers, rare, onto the grill.

The sizzling sound that they make interacts nicely with the two steak sandwiches that are already cooking. Lots of fries already cooked, maybe we need some more burgers from the refrigerator. Time to turn the steaks and the rare cheeseburgers. Take the order for five burgers, all rare, hold the pickles and onions on three of 'em! Don't try and remember any of this. When they're cooked just look up at the face and it will all come rushing back to you. Do you want any fries with this, sir? Turn the burgers, dress the buns, take an order, dump the fries, make up a hot dog, turn those steaks, turn those burgers, salt them down, take the fries out of the grease. (I'm gonna have to change that grease pretty soon). Take an order, and another, and one more. Dress the buns, hold the pickles and onions on those three for the fat guy with acne. Do you want any fries with that, sir?

Usually the restaurant was busy and I didn't notice the customers that much. They were nameless faces who ordered burgers. The permutations of their orders fascinated me. In a year of cooking four nights a week, I must have prepared over 35,000 burgers, 750,000 french fries, 3,000 hot dogs, and 10,000 steak sandwiches.

Every once in a while somebody would come in and watch me cook. They would have a pleased expression on their face that said, "Hey! You're an artist and your burgers are your art...you are damn good at your job and I love to watch you work."

□

For two years I worked as a laboratory assistant in a large blood bank. My workmate was R. L. Jones.

R. L. Jones's wit and wisdom was illustrative of the type of brilliance that Thelonius Monk had in mind when he said, "Every man is a genius at being himself." R. L. certainly was. He was one of the most intelligent, yet ignorant men that I have ever met. He could have taken on any of the guys from my medical school class in poker or dice and separated them from their money faster than they could have said "chronic obstructive pulmonary disease" (COPD). He was clever, irreverent, lazy, hysterically funny, and rarely sober. After an initial feeling-out period on the job, we got to be good friends. I am recording some of his wisdom here for future generations to reflect upon.

During my initial job interview I was told that the most challenging aspect of my new position would be dealing with "R. L." I got myself ready for a mean old guy as I heard story after story about R. L. terrorizing coworkers, chasing women in the halls at work, and coming to the job under the influence of alcohol. These stories all turned out to be true.

No story in the world could have properly prepared me for our introductory meeting. R. L. had a Fu Manchu mustache and goatee, a rat's nest of conked, blue-tinted hair combed back in a pompadour, and a handshake the consistency of yesterday's tuna casserole. I couldn't tell if he was black or Chinese, or Martian, or what. He was wearing a beautiful pair of pointy alligator shoes that must have been at least thirty years old. He had a cigarette dangling from his mouth, and he gave me a suspicious glare before moving on.

In my first five minutes on the job, R. L. taught me everything I needed to know. The tubes come off the truck, serums go up to Labeling, pop off the corks, spin them down for ten, make that eight, oh shit, six minutes will do it, pour off the plasma and deliver them to Antibody Screening. R. L. had done this same work for almost thirty years. Same job, same building, same workbench. Bosses would come and go, other workers would come and go, and he knew that I, too, would come and go. I figured I'd be lucky to last two weeks.

We received a load of new tubes approximately once every hour. Between the two of us, we could handle any amount of specimens in ten minutes. This left the lion's share of the shift for the Laker game on television, meals pilfered from the lab's kitchen, and plenty of studying on my part to try and ensure entrance into medical school. Somehow two weeks stretched out into two years. R. L. turned out to be a wonderful character and conversationalist. We had a lot of good times on the job.

I present a sample of some of R. L.'s finer moments and some of his more acute reflections on life.

ON HIS JOB: One night R. L. came to work about an hour late, as was his habit. He then disappeared for the next two hours. We both had access to a schedule, and he knew that no tubes were coming in during this period of time. Out of curiosity more than anything else, I tracked him down. He was way off in the plasmapheresis room. He was lounging in a big comfortable blood donor's chair watching the Laker game on the lab's color TV. I was angry that he hadn't shared his fun with me and I started to jive him about not doing any work.

"Jim," he said. "You've just got to understand something about our job. It is exactly the same as being a doctor." He went on in all seriousness. "When my patients don't come in, I can't do no work!" R. L., you're right, yeah, I just never looked at it like that before. I began to give serious thought as to why I was working so hard to get into medical school.

ON SEX: "Hypersexual" does not begin to describe R. L.'s obsession with the female gender. I doubt if the man went fifteen minutes during a work shift without mentioning women, or fondling his testicles, or making a grab at mine.

ON LANGUAGE AND R. L.'S NAME: R. L. rarely stopped talking. He had a remarkable facility for adapting the vagaries of language to his special needs. For example, one night we were driving around town together and he said, "Hey, bro'. How 'bout puttin' some glass in that hole!" Translation: Please close the window.

"I'm constipating." Translation: I'm concentrating, I'm busy.

White people were "ofays," "pales," or "blanks." Jews were "Youish." Our Filipino coworkers were "Pipinos," "Pineapples," or "Filopenises." New employees were "fish." Everybody in the world was either a "mother," or a "mothergrabber."

This need of R. L.'s to subvert the language probably was rooted in his very first days. R. L. was foaled on an Indian reservation. His father was Creole and his mother was a Cherokee. They named their first son "Earl" which somehow got transferred to the birth certificate as "R. L." R. L. became the man's handle, for better or for worse.

R. L. had created an alternate persona that he only utilized on the telephone. This was "Pierre Smith." Whenever he left a telephone message anywhere, he would use that name. Even with people he trusted, even when calling his wife! He never explained why.

Besides being quotable, R. L. was simply the most outrageous man I have ever known. The lab where we worked was part of a large charitable organization. They maintained a long-standing policy of not firing any employee who had put in more than twenty-five years of service. R. L. had done some "hard time" at his job, almost thirty years' worth. He knew that the lab's retirement policy placed him squarely in the driver's seat. On the anniversary of his twenty-fifth year of work, R. L. had taken a trip down the hall to the lab's administration offices. He had told them in no uncertain terms that they should get his retirement papers ready to be signed. He might be quitting any day. That was almost five years ago! Hardly a week went by without R. L. discussing his imminent retirement.

R. L.'s knowledge that he could retire comfortably at any time gave him a sense of personal freedom. He was capable of the most extraordinary behavior on the job.

He showed little compunction about discussing elaborate sexual fantasies in front of the Filipino Seventh Day Adventists who shared our work space. He would inflame them with his racism and sexism. He would sleep on the job, and generally do everything he could to avoid work. He would conveniently be ill on any day with a heavy workload.

He was a rascal, and I liked him immensely. He was honest and funny and he never shut up. He taught me many things. He was so negative, such a misanthrope, so open, so disarming that I just had to love the guy....

Three years after I quit my job with R.L, I returned to visit the old goat. I came late in his shift and took him out to a bar for his favorite drink, Christian Brothers brandy and grapefruit juice.

It was wonderful to see him again. He talked on and on about the job, his imminent retirement, women, what a shame it was that I had gotten a tumor, and how rotten the job had become without somebody to pal around with. The "new guy," who had replaced me three years before, never ditched work, or joked, or fooled around. R. L. couldn't get too serious about this job—after all, he might retire any day.

I left the bar feeling very sad. I drove around the neighborhood and looked at all of the crappy places where R. L. and I had eaten together. The only decent place, a Greek restaurant that served incredible lamb on a bountiful dish of rice pilaf, had become "Choy's Chinese and American." Now I was even sadder.

I had changed a lot. The neighborhood had changed a little bit. But R. L. really wasn't much different. He was going to wake up, smoke, drink, work, crack jokes, and act crazy each and every day. It didn't matter to him who he worked with, or whether or not my cancer was malignant, or whether or not Poland was invaded, or whether or not there was life on Venus. He operated on a different scale. A change of clerks at the corner store was an event of cosmic proportions in his life. I guess that we are all similar. Nothing much changes except the scale.

I went over to "Sam's All-American Burger." I munched my burger out on the patio. It was a warm, muggy L.A. evening but the smog had lifted and the air felt fresh. I watched the lights of the big downtown buildings twinkling, and I thought a lot about constancy and change, and cancer, and Sam's burgers. They tasted exactly as they had three years ago. Sam looked the same, too. He had a horse to bet on the next day that was a "sure thing." He told me that he would be a very rich man if it came in. I asked him what he would do with all of his money if he suddenly became very wealthy.

"I dunno..." he answered. "But I can tell ya one thing, ya wouldn't catch me cooking these frigging burgers any more!"

Lots of burgers. And horses coming down the stretch in an improbable order that will make Sam a rich man. Sam will lend me some of his new wealth and I'll be a rich man. I might become so rich that I could cure myself of cancer. Sure I could! Or I could just take all of my money and fly somewhere far away like China or Cuba. Or I could spend it all on brandy and grapefruit juice.

Then I remembered that I was still at Sam's. Now I was extremely sad. Constancy and change. Constancy and change. Constancy and change. And cancer. Always cancer.

CHAPTER SEVEN

Medical School

Oh, yeah, I had my dreams and illusions about the whole thing. I wanted it to be exciting and eye-opening. I wanted to unlock some of the mysteries, to come closer to the great secrets of life and death. I wanted it to be fascinating and conceptual. I hoped it would be stimulating and challenging. Instead it turned out to be dull and forgettable: an unending procession of facts, charts, tables, words, values, and names to be memorized. It was just like all of the other school experiences I had waded through to get into medicine. Few of the right questions were posed, the premises were wrong. Somebody had built the whole system on top of a false premise. I felt as if I was in a free fall from grace. I had bitten into the apple and it would be my undoing. But I couldn't remember when I had taken that first bite—what did I do to deserve this?

And then there were the people. My fellow students. I had allowed myself great illusions about them as well. Some part of me hoped for a cadre of committed activists, people who were interested in the important social questions that their future profession was facing. Instead, I found a very distinct group of people who loved to study, take notes, go to lectures, and buy books. The guys loved sports and the beach. The girls liked the guys and the beach. What was I doing here? How would I ever make it through four years of this?

Medical school seemed like it would begin innocuously enough. The first day of school was Orientation Day, designed to provide the student with the opportunity to meet the people that he or she would be hanging out with for the next four years.

Orientation Day began with a talk by the dean of the medical school, Dr. D. His rousing and inspiring discussion of the path that we were about to embark upon bored me to tears. He was followed on the dais by a procession of assistant deans. Each managed to reiterate Dr. D.'s speech in a slightly different way. Dr. O. was the special guest star. I knew him from my undergraduate days. He had made a name for himself with his work on the effects of LSD upon the central nervous systems of elephants. The story I heard was that Dr. O. had mistakenly based his dosage calculations on the total body weight of the elephant, rather than on the brain weight of the beast. A test elephant was given his dose of acid with a hypodermic gun. Immediately after receiving the injection, the poor elephant walked around in a half circle for about ten seconds and then keeled over—dead as a doornail.

Dr. O. was a rotund, jolly-looking fellow with a cinder block for a head, and an irrepressible smile on his face. He actually carried a marble bust of Hippocrates up on stage with him. He began his talk with a period of silence during which he stared at the bust and caressed its furrowed brow. "This...is the...face...of a...worried ...man," he intoned.

I took the opportunity to scrutinize the faces of my fellow classmates as they soaked up Dr. O's speech. They were young, clean, and boring. Some of my classmates were busily taking notes. Dr. O. was rolling now, but he wasn't saying anything worth writing down. It was going to be a long four years.

The day ended with a series of skits put on by the second-year students. My classmates roared appreciatively. The show ended with the entire class singing "Mama, Don't Let Your Sons Grow Up to Be Doctors." I wanted to cry. Early that evening I attended the Orientation Day party. I tried to talk to as many different students as I could. I began downing wine coolers to stave off the depression I now felt. With each new classmate I met, my spirits sagged lower and lower. It was going to be an alcoholic four years!

The first group I approached was deeply involved in a discussion about mortgage rates. They were talking about how their parents manipulated their low interest educational loans. Some used them as down payments on condominiums for their little princes and princesses. I fought off a rising tide of nausea with a couple more wine coolers. I moved on to a group of men who were discussing...you guessed it...sports and women. Don't get me wrong. I don't mind talking about sports. My friend Joe can discuss boxing with an appreciation for the sport and a clarity of insight that is quite stimulating. But these guys, oh, Jesus—these guys could even make the World Series seem boring. As I inhaled a few more wine coolers I began to understand why doctors had such horrible drug problems. They bored each other to death! In a desperate search for stimulation they turned to drugs.

I tried several more forays into the crowd. Each time the conversations drove me quickly back to the safety of the wine. One group of kids was discussing the Bible. "Hey, let's set up a Bible study group,..." "Yeah, great idea!" A group of guys were comparing football teams of their undergraduate alma maters. What a great bunch of guys! Go Michigan, go Notre Dame, go Wolverines, go Fighting Irish, go, go, go! Go! Go! Go home, Jim! After a few more wine coolers that's exactly what I did.

□

Orientation was only the beginning. Class social events were so depressing for me that I stopped attending. I kept hoping that things would get better once I got to know some of these people. For the most part, I was disappointed.

Take G.W., for example. He lived and breathed medicine. He had wanted to be a doctor as far back as he could remember. His first words as an infant had been "autoimmune deficiency disease," and he had spent every summer since kindergarten volunteering in a cardiology laboratory. After originally being rejected by UCLA, as well as all of the other med schools to which he had applied, he began collecting data on the minority students who'd been accepted. He asked these kids for their test scores and grade point averages. When he saw that their qualifications were similar to his, he went totally "freaky-deaky." Another classmate told me that he had seen G.W. in the library ethnic data collection that day. G.W. was sitting alone, acting like a nut. He was breaking pencils while repeating over and over to himself, "It's not fair... it's just not fair...." The poor guy was crying like a baby, and not even his best friends consoled him. Within a week, G.W.'s parents had hired a lawyer and G.W. was threatening the medical school administration with a reverse discrimination suit. The school acquiesced and let him in.

G.W. was bad, but there were worse. There was Y.A. Oh, what the hell, I'm going to go ahead and spell out his name! He can sue my estate because I'll probably be dead by the time he reads this, and his name is important. It was Yitz, and he was such a standout fool that his name became transformed into a noun. A Yitz, an idiot, a jerk, a buffoon. Yitz was easily the loudest student at orientation. He ran around like a chicken with his head cut off, telling jokes, hustling the women indiscriminately, and immediately establishing himself as a clown of monumental proportions. The first day of classes he again demonstrated his individuality by roller-skating into morning lecture. A few weeks later he began to wear a yarmulke to school. He told me he was studying the Torah on weekends and that it was just as exciting as his medical school studies.

I was diagnosed as having a brain tumor in the summer between my first and second year of medical school. At this time I was treated with radiation therapy to my brain. I returned to school completely bald as a result of the heavy dose of radiation. Yitz was one of the first students to come up to me and ask what was going on. I explained that I had received radiation treatment for a brain tumor. He responded quite nicely and seemed sincerely concerned. He hoped that everything would work out well, and he promised to pray for me whenever he could. Two days later he was back in my face again, asking about my "cyst." I patiently and clearly explained that my problem was not a "cyst." It was a tumor with a capital T. Once again he responded warmly. When the schmuck started asking about my "cyst" again a few days later, I lost my temper. Three strikes and you're out, Yitz! I told him one last time that I had been treated for a tumor, not a cyst. I told him that I wanted to break his neck, but doing that would only reinforce his desire to speak with me again. I wanted to avoid that at all costs. "So please stay the hell away from me and don't ever speak to me again unless I address you first!" Yitz and I never spoke again.

The issue here is much more critical than simple consideration or politeness. Here was someone who was studying to be a doctor. This guy was planning to spend his entire workday attending to other people's health care needs. Yet he didn't have the most basic prerequisite for this activity: he didn't know how to listen. Yitz and G.W. were advanced cases with poor prognoses—although they were by no means the only maladapted personalities in my class. Some of the nicer people bagged the whole thing after a few weeks. It just wasn't their cup of tea. The flakiest people seemed to be the ones who thrived in this environment. Like flies around shit.

□

There were one hundred and fifty students in my class. By the end of the first year I had found about ten whom I would trust to do even the simplest medical procedure. Few of the people in my class were competent. The mature student was the exception. There was T. F., a mother of three, a professional midwife, and an articulate, intelligent socialist. There was V. H., father of two boys, who had done relief work in Latin America, and who held down two graveyard shifts a week at the local 7-Eleven to put himself through medical school. And A. Z., a Leninist who became my roommate, and watched from the sidelines as my brain lost the big game against cancer.

By and large my classmates were an exceptionally lame bunch of people. These kids were too clean, too lily-white, too eager to please for my taste. They were sheltered, young, and unaffected by the world around them. Most of them had absolutely no common sense. Few had any interesting life experiences. They were the type of kids who had studied their way through high school and college. They had spent all of their summers and vacations working in some research laboratory. For them, final exams week was a peak experience.

I finally saw that the curriculum and the medical school students complemented each other perfectly. The students were timid about taking control of their lives. Medical school provided the control—everything is predetermined, all of the important decisions have already been made. Their lives were filled to the brim with lectures, exams, practicals, review sessions, tutorials... they had no time for the big questions as they attempted to master the massive amount of trivia in the medical school curriculum. New ideas are time consuming.

Medical school is a confusing, mind-numbing experience designed to fill every neuron of the student's brain with data of questionable relevance. There is little time for the student to grow as a human being. The atmosphere of the classroom is charged with competition. This is fine for the majority of students who approach school exclusively as a measure of their self-worth. The workload is enormous. There is absolutely no time to evaluate what is important in the program. The student is faced with three choices: either try and learn everything, or try and learn just enough to get by, or learn what is obviously interesting and relevant and flunk out of school. Most students attempt to learn everything. I chose to learn only enough to get by.

Medical school is an exercise in arbitrary and capricious authority. "You will do this because I say you will do this!" I had an especially violent reaction to this aspect of school. Most of the other kids thrived in this environment. I'm not sure what made me different. Perhaps my previous experiences with authoritarian bosses on the job, or the childhood battles with my dad, or simply the fact that I was a few years older than most of the other students. I hated going to school every day and taking directions from a bunch of pencil-pushing academics.

Near the end of our first quarter we got a valuable lesson in medical school politics. A group of students decided they wanted to change the test date of one of our final exams. The test was in Biostatistics, the least emphasized course in our bloated curriculum. The Biostatistics professors were completely amenable to the change, as was the head of the Statistics Department and all of the deans of the medical school. We assumed that we had covered all our bases, and there would be no problem in changing the test date. Enter Dr. K.

I knew of Dr. K. through a friend of mine who worked in his research lab. Dr. K. had been a hotshot resident in internal medicine when a medical condition put him on the disabled list. He was farmed out to the milder pastures of academia—teaching and research. He dropped in on us following one of our Anatomy lectures. He wanted to discuss our proposal to change the Biostatistics exam date. He told us that he understood our concerns. Five final exams in one week was a tough schedule. Yes, he was aware that we had gone through all of the proper channels to get the date changed. However, he was here today representing the medical school's Educational Curriculum Committee. Our final exam dates had been set years ago and we couldn't change them now. He said he appreciated our interest in the curriculum. Any questions?

Yeah, Dr. K., I've got one big fat question: Why can't we change the test date? You can't because you can't because you can't. Blah blah, uh, er, blah, blah, blah. You just can't. You can't because I said so, I'll be happy to discuss it further, out in the hall.

If Dr. K. had hoped that the whole thing would just die down by the time we got out to the hall, he was sorely mistaken. About twenty of the more fanatical students on both sides of the issue were out there, ready to meet him when he rolled up, coffee in hand. He told us that he would be happy to listen to all opinions, but please, let's have them one at a time. T. M., a cheerful guy who wore

Hawaiian shirts to school and worked out everyone's astrological charts in his spare time, didn't like how the whole thing was polarizing the class. He mumbled something inane about the "negativity" the issue was causing. He urged Dr. K. to come to a decision, any decision, so we could go on without all of this horrible dissension. Dr. K. sipped his coffee and nodded approvingly.

S. F. spoke next. She was one of the students who had organized the whole affair. She hadn't meant to cause any problems for anyone. She hoped that the new test date would make life a little easier for us. She didn't see what the big stink was all about.

Dr. K. continued to sip his coffee. He was listening attentively.

D. E. had the floor next. He was from the Deep South and drawled out his concern about the issue. The arrogance of his fellow classmates who wanted to change the exam date was "downright disturbing." Their behavior made him want to apologize on behalf of the entire class. A small group of "instigators" was making a big deal out of nothing. D. E. was embarrassed. Here we were, first-year students, acting like we knew what was good for us and wasting Dr. K.'s precious time.

At this point I could no longer hold my tongue. What do you mean, wasting his time? He's getting paid for this! Aren't you Dr. K.? I rambled on about how we, the students, had too little control of the educational process, and that the damn school should be there for our needs, and the damn curriculum should be adjusted for us, and we kept the whole thing going with our goddam tuition and we paid Dr. K.'s goddam salary, and he should be working for us instead of being an obstruction to us.

Dr. K. stopped drinking his coffee. He looked like a man who suddenly needed something stronger. All of the blood had left his face and he was unconsciously clenching and unclenching his jaw. Finally he sputtered, "Young man...that is unadulterated bullshit!" Then he turned on his heel and walked away.

We ended up writing a petition signed by virtually every member of the class. The date was changed to reflect our wishes.

After this incident there was some brave talk among the students about how we should start preparing to change the following year's curriculum. We had a meeting or two, but these efforts never amounted to much. People were too busy trying to survive the onslaught of the first year curriculum to worry about changing the second. With all of the tests, lectures, practicals, etc., the student was lucky to have time to change underwear, much less the educational curriculum.

Medical school is a factory. Like any other factory, its purpose is to turn out finished products. In this case, the product is a doctor—a clean, refinished, high-gloss guy or gal ready to go out in the world, heal the sick, and raise the dead! For me, though, life was too short to spend it in those damn lecture halls. Many classes I stopped attending altogether. I would utilize this time to study at home. I then had a few nights a week completely free. I volunteered every week at the Los Angeles Free Clinic. The staff there is compassionate and dedicated. The medical care is high quality and free of charge to everyone. After a week of school, the Free Clinic was a breath of fresh air. I would leave there with a feeling of, *Yeah, this is what I want to do with my life! Give some medical attention to the folks who can't afford private doctors or medical insurance.*

I never thought I would be in need of care. Medical student, heal thyself.

CHAPTER EIGHT

Dealing with the Doctors

I HAD ALWAYS ENTERTAINED THE VAGUE NOTION that I would enjoy perpetual good health. After all, I was on my way to medical school. I was going to be a hot-shot doctor, and we all know that doctors never get sick. I jogged four miles a day with regularity, had good eating habits, and I didn't ingest any recreational drugs. I had never taken medications of any kind. My body always responded whenever I needed it. I was only twenty-five years old; it would have been inappropriate for me to have any worries about my health. Little did I suspect how rudely my adolescent fantasy of immortality would be shattered. About a week before medical school began, I started to experience double vision. I remember running after a ball in the outfield during my weekly softball game and seeing two balls coming at me. I don't remember being particularly frightened. *There must be something wrong with my eye—what a drag! Maybe it's my glasses....*

Dr. G. was the first physician to have the pleasure of attending to my problem. He was the same gruff old man who had been fitting me for glasses since I was a kid. If I had only known then how many members of the "help-ing professions" (nurses, doctors, physicians' assistants, residents, etc.) would follow Dr. G.'s lead and poke, turn, touch, test, torture, treat, photograph, probe, and radiate the various orifices and areas of my body. . . . If I had known how long this road would be. *If I had only known!*

Dr. G.'s conclusion was close to the truth. Certainly it was as helpful as any of the other judgments I would receive that year. He thought I was suffering from a nutritional deficiency. He yelled at me to start taking vitamins. As I was leaving, he mumbled something about how I should get some medical insurance that would cover a neurology examination. Megadoses of vitamins, the therapy recommended by Dr. G., failed to do much more than give me gas and turn my urine a deep orange color.

Dr. S., my family's general practitioner, was my next advisor. He spent forty-five minutes explaining to me how he had been tricked into going to medical school by his parents. He had always wanted to be a pharmacist. He gave me a complete physical exam, including an EKG and my very first rectal. The EKG demonstrated that I had an obscure heart syndrome that had absolutely no clinical significance. The rectal left my anus feeling sore, and I was left wondering what the connection was between my eye and my asshole.

Looking back on that first visit to Dr. S., I realize that it contained an important lesson about modern medicine. Our doctors' ability to diagnose far surpasses their knowledge of therapy. I was told by Dr. S. that I had a heartbeat pattern on the EKG machine that was "Very interesting. A borderline Wolff-Parkinson-White pattern."

Wow! A real syndrome, a pattern! "What does it mean, Dr. S?" I was excited. We might have picked up the trail of my problem.

"Nothing. Do you ever get tachycardia (fast heart beats)?"

"Well, no."

"Then it means absolutely nothing. It's just a pattern."

Dr. S.'s little diagnostic device allowed him to identify a totally meaningless pattern that had no bearing on my problem. His training had prodded him into mentioning it unnecessarily. I thank God that there was nothing he could do to treat it, or else I would have suffered the consequences. Dr. S. ended the exam by saying that I probably had this eye problem at birth and I was just beginning to notice it! I was flabbergasted. This was the first of many comments I received from doctors implying that my problem was psychological in origin. Because I had symptoms that couldn't be diagnosed or treated, doctors assumed that the problem was all in my mind. I left his office feeling strangely unattended. He had recommended a CAT scan of my brain. I tried to reconcile his statement about the problem being congenital with the need for a CAT scan, which I knew was used to find brain tumors. Now I was scared. I knew that Dr. S. was incorrect about my having had this problem since childhood. I knew he actually had no idea about what was wrong with my eye. If he couldn't figure it out, who could?

I only vaguely remember my first CAT scan. I have since had at least ten more and have decided that I will, under no circumstances, have another. I'm sure that bored, efficient technicians, wearing pastel-colored uniforms with little name tags and happy face buttons, were on hand. I'm sure the machine made a noise somewhat akin to the whirring of a washing machine. I'm sure that I was cooperative as a log, and very pleasant to the nurses. I'm sure that I hated the intravenous iodine dripping warmly into my arm vein, making me nauseous and ferociously aware of my need to pee.

My CAT scan turned out to be completely normal, but I knew that I was getting more and more ill with each passing day. Some strange intuition made me focus on the belief that I had a brain tumor. I now think that even people who are medically ignorant can be very accurate diagnosticians for themselves. At the very least, they can predict with unerring accuracy the severity of their problem. Doctors could save themselves time and trouble if they would ask their patients two questions, "What do you think is going on?" and "How serious do you feel your problem is?" The answers would be shockingly close to the truth. I knew intuitively that I had a brain tumor six months before the doctors finally caught on.

Dr. D. worked with Dr. B. at a children's medical center. Both were experts in eye problems. They had some new theories. Maybe I had multiple sclerosis and, then again, maybe I had myasthenia gravis. The wonderful thing about myasthenia gravis was that they could do a test for it right there in the office that same afternoon! They quickly produced one of the scores of complex medical consent forms that I signed without reading. Then they injected a drug into my arm. They told me that nothing would happen if I did not have the disease and so, for about thirty seconds, I felt relieved because nothing happened. All of a sudden, I noticed that Dr. B. looked like he was sitting about ten miles away and I was getting extremely hot and tired and nauseated and it became very foggy and.... plop! My head went down and I passed out.

I could have saved myself a lot of agony by remaining unconscious for the next two years. Instead, I woke up a few moments later and noticed that Dr. B. had come back and was extremely close to me. He was acting very nervous as he put some kind of antidote into my arm. I felt so nauseated and groggy that I wanted to die, right there in that office filled with toys and dolls and Captain Kangaroo posters. What a nice place to die! Dr. B. informed me that I had just experienced a negative test. The drug would have made me feel wonderfully strong if I had myasthenia gravis, and it certainly didn't do that.

Both of the good doctors ruled out multiple sclerosis on the basis of my clinical picture. After a hushed conference outside the examining room, they told me that I probably had a virus affecting my sixth cranial nerve, and that most likely it would clear up on its own time. Dr. D. then recommended his "very good friend at UCLA, Dr. T., who is a specialist in your type of problem." He added that it wouldn't hurt to see a neurologist.

Now I was really worried. This business about a virus . . . I didn't know much about doctors at this early stage of my illness, but I knew enough to be suspicious about any diagnosis of a virus. Viruses are elusive characters. They are very small and extremely hard to grow outside of the body. Doctors cannot even decide if viruses are alive or not, much less diagnose or treat them. I knew that I had just been handed a diagnosis by default. "Whenever it can't be anything else, assume that it's a virus."

Dr. G. was a neurologist with a good reputation. He was known by my family, as well. I don't remember much of what he did during my examination. I know he asked me about venereal disease, and my "participation in the drug scene." At the time I didn't see the connection, but he must have felt that I was burning up with tertiary syphilis or that I was slowly cooking my neurons with some exotic drugs. He had no idea as to what was causing my eye problem.

Meanwhile, Dr. T. (Dr. D.'s "good friend") turned out to be a cornea specialist—a field totally removed from my area of concern. He said that the person I should see was Dr. N., who truly did have expertise with my problem. Not only was he an "eye movement specialist," but he had actually seen cases like mine before. Dr. T. didn't seem to be very worried about my life span.

Dr. N. was a very nice man, very warm. He exuded confidence. He didn't know exactly why my eye was not working but he had a name for the syndrome: "right sixth cranial nerve paresis." He was the first of many doctors to say, "We'll find the solution to your problem."

"Every medical problem has an optimal solution." If I only knew then how many times I would hear this refrain, this litany, over and over, again and again. The world is a rational place, right? Every problem can be solved, right? Eventually, I would figure out that there simply is no medical solution to my problem, but only after a long bout with this disease. Had I known this basic fact two years ago with the certainty that I have now, I would have spared myself a great deal of false hope. I definitely could have avoided the headaches of dealing with the medical establishment. Had there been a doctor, just one, with the fortitude to be honest with me, I could have saved myself a lot of unnecessary anguish. But at this point, I was on a fervent quest, a quest to eliminate what I was certain was a tumor.

Dr. N. phoned me excitedly one day. He had asked a radiologist to reexamine my original CAT scan. The radiologist observed "a definite area of abnormality" that indicated I had a benign tumor of the pituitary gland. This growth could be removed surgically with a procedure that would involve going in through my nose! Dr. N. was very happy about the diagnosis. He told me that there could be many different reasons for my double vision: a pituitary tumor was one of the few things that was curable. Dr. N. referred me to a neurosurgeon, Dr. I. Dr. I. didn't see anything abnormal on the CAT scan. He ordered another, "special" CAT scan along with some other X-rays, which were called tomograms. All of the new tests were completely normal. None of the good doctors knew what to do.

As a present for being accepted into medical school, my parents had bought me a year's subscription to the *New England Journal of Medicine.* I knew it would be inappropriate at this early stage of my education to concern myself with the details in each article, but I thought it would be a good idea to read one article a week to absorb basic medical terminology. The first issue arrived soon after my consultation with Dr. I. I noticed with interest something called a "case report" and turned to it. To my utter shock and disbelief, the man the article was describing had the exact same symptoms as I did! (By this time I had developed ringing in my right ear and a twitch in my right eyelid.) I anxiously read over the article. I didn't understand most of the medical jargon but I painstakingly translated it into English, using my new medical dictionary. The poor patient in the article had a *pontine glioma*—the exact diagnosis I ended up with.

How could I possibly know that the words in the article, which were then so foreign, e.g. *nystagmus, dysarthria, dysphagia, paretic*, etc., would soon be as familiar to me as my car's interior. These words would become a part of my daily life, thoughts, and vocabulary. They would even enter the lives of those close to me. I studied the article carefully for an indication of prognosis or treatment. I saw only the cold sentence, "A surgical treatment was performed." A surgical treatment? What the hell does that mean? Did it work? Was the guy cured? I was ready to hit the operating table right then and there. Put me to sleep and cut it out!

Neither Dr. N. nor Dr. I. seemed very concerned about the article. Neither of them had read it. Dr. N. said that he was convinced I was going through "medical school-itis: you're just imagining you have every disease you read about." Dr. I. insisted that I "could not have a brain tumor. There's nothing on the brain . . . nothing. I looked at your CAT scan myself!"

In my case, diagnostic possibilities were tossed around like juggling pins. Maybe it's this and maybe it's that, and maybe it's a little of this and that, and we've got to consider this and that possibility, but we can rule that out. Diagnoses flew through the air with the greatest of ease, but when it came time for treatment—wham! Down slammed the doors of scientific rationality.

Suddenly the doctors were on Quaaludes, everything got stuck on slow speed, the whole process was moving so slowly. Over the next few months, nothing happened with the doctors. I kept getting sicker and sicker. Finally, during the last week of my first year of medical school, I began to crumble neurologically. I had to enter the hospital.

I tried to talk my doctors into letting me stay out of the hospital for one more week. I wanted to finish the academic year. But the doctors were nervous about having me out on the streets. My doubts about my need for hospitalization were quickly dispelled by my last pre-hospital meal. My true love, Laurie, offered to take me out to the restaurant of my choice. Los Angeles has many nice restaurants and I'm sure she expected me to choose one of them. After all, this might be my last taste of real world food for quite some time. When I opted for a local barbecue joint, she became convinced that I really had suffered severe brain damage. While sampling my order of ribs, it became even more evident that I should get to the hospital, pronto. I couldn't swallow the meat! Hey, this was serious!

□

My experiences in doctors' offices hardly prepared me for the agonies that exist on the neurological ward of a hospital. There was no question that I was in need of some help. By the time I finally checked in, I couldn't move my right eye at all, my face was paralyzed on the right side, I couldn't swallow, I had trouble walking, and I couldn't feel anything on the left side of my body.

Coming onto the ward, I was immediately confronted by the head nurse.

"Where have you been? We expected you two hours ago!"

This pleasant welcome was immediately followed by a set of commands. I was to strip, dress in hospital pajamas, get into bed—and stay there. Just be a good patient.

It is difficult to express the cumulative effect that a few weeks of hospital life can have on a person's feelings of self-esteem. The patient starts from a position of being one-down. He is in a weakened and/or dependent physical state. He is then subjected to a daily routine of doctors who say nothing, pastel-colored food, which isn't nutritious or satisfying to the taste, roommates with serious illnesses, inconclusive tests, the drone of the ever-present TV, and the hollow clanging sounds that go on endlessly in the hall. I thought I was unlucky because I always ended up with a room right at the epicenter of the clanging. I finally figured out that the clanging is everywhere—no matter where one's room is.

I will never forget the hateful smells, the military regimentation, the boredom, the lack of human warmth, and the aura of bustling efficiency that I now know hides a million errors—large and small. I will never forget the lack of stimuli and the stagnant sense of death that hangs heavily in the halls. I will never forget the unnecessary intrusions on my time and body, the feeling of imminent danger, the removal of my individuality, the presence of uniforms, and the metallic emptiness of a world completely dominated by machinery.

My brain turned out to be a very difficult area to assess medically. I remember my first stay in the hospital as a montage of barbarities inflicted upon me by the neuroradiology department. They injected radioactive contrast material into my veins. Then they injected it into my spinal column. Then they injected special fluorescent dye into my spine. None of these efforts produced a clear view of my troubles. They finally resorted to the "old-fashioned" technique of injecting air right into my addled brain. Each technique promised a better picture than the last. None of these photographs proved to be definitive. Nobody would make a diagnosis. I began to suspect that the doctors were trying to kill me so that they could do an autopsy and find out, with assurance, what was wrong with me. For a while, I rationalized this fear away as paranoia induced by stress. Then, a friend of mine with an incurable disease related how his doctors had discussed what the pathologists were planning to do with his body at his imminent autopsy, right in front of him.

The most vivid aspect of this first hospitalization was the amazing amount of contradiction between the opinions of the different doctors. Luckily, my family and friends are intelligent and patient. They were more than willing to sit with me for a few hours each night and attempt to unravel the garbled mass of information that we heard each day. Every doctor, resident, intern, orderly, nurse, and janitor seemed to have an opinion about my case. Part of this little game involved trying to figure out exactly how much each person really knew, and therefore how much weight to give each opinion.

The janitors knew the most. After a quick glance one of them told me, "Shit, you're pretty messed up for a young man!"

Looking back, I realize that most of the medical people wouldn't have recognized a *pontine glioma* unless it was riding home on the bus next to them. Even then they would have some "other ideas," "diagnostic possibilities," "remote potentialities," "needs to rule out," etc.

Dr. C. walked into the midst of this morass one Saturday morning. He was a well-known private neurologist. I felt nervous about seeing him. I didn't want to ruffle the professional feathers of the university physicians who had been working on my case. I thought they might get upset by my family's desire for an outside opinion. Also I didn't think that any new doctor would be able to add anything at this point. However, my parents had heard great things about Dr. C. and convinced him to pick up the scent.

Dr. C. took almost two hours to complete his neurological assessment. This was partially because he was so thorough and partially because he was severely crippled from childhood polio. His was the most complete examination I had ever undergone. When he was finished, he laboriously wrote up a note in my chart. His evaluation was complete with neurologic findings, a diagram of the tumor he suspected I had, a sequential listing of the minimum number of neuroradiologic tests I should undergo in order to rule out other diagnostic possibilities, and all of the treatments to be considered if his diagnosis proved correct. He then announced succinctly and carefully, in the presence of my family and friends, that I probably had a brain tumor with the name *pontine glioma*, and that it had been his experience that these tumors were radiosensitive, i.e., responded well to radiation therapy. Period.

I felt as if I had been jolted by an electric current. Five days of dealing with the death merchants of the hospital had weakened my resolve to the point where I assumed that I would never live to be treated. In fact, I had begun to give up hope that I would live long enough to be diagnosed. I was even beginning to wonder whether my whole problem was neurotic in nature. Could I have been making the whole thing up? Not if it had a name, not if I could get a doctor to believe that it was serious. Dr. C.'s diagnosis was a beautiful thing to hear, and I rejoiced inside. I was ecstatic that there was actually a treatment for my problem. I even put aside my nagging fear as to how everyone else could have been so unclear, while Dr. C. had gotten right to the point so easily.

The other doctors coming in on Monday were impressed with Dr. C.'s assessments but didn't reveal much surprise about his clarity. I half expected at least one person to say, "Yeah, wow!... That's quite clear, a nice synthesis of your clinical picture." I awaited some indication from my doctors that would tell me that a week of their frantic bumbling over my ass, with all of their fancy technology, had produced less than a single competent neurologic exam. Instead, my doctors seemed to take on Dr. C.'s analysis as their own. I'm sure they would have reached the same conclusion on their own... eventually.

Dr. C.'s diagnosis withstood the test of time. After another week in the hospital nobody could come up with anything better. The doctors decided that radiation therapy was to be the next stage of my life. I must say that it wasn't terribly bad. No pain involved, treatments took less than two minutes each day, and there were no major side effects except hair loss and lassitude. After one year of seeing doctors, I was happy that I had finally been offered a diagnosis. The fact that there was a treatment for my disease was an added bonus.

I never seriously questioned whether or not to receive radiation. The fact that it was so easy to undergo reinforced in my mind the idea that it was the proper thing to do. But the sad fact of the matter is, with cancers of the brain, radiation therapy usually doesn't work. It did give me a wonderful six months of moderately normal living, for which I will be eternally grateful. It also made me falsely believe that I had beaten cancer. Now I find myself with a tumor much worse than my original one, right back in the same place. I am left with the feelings of having been hoodwinked, of having participated in someone else's fantasy, and of not having been in control of my fate.

During the entire course of therapy I was haunted by the feeling that my radiation therapist had made a technical error in the design of my radiation protocol. My initial consultation with Dr. E. had not gone well. He was a nice man, but had a tendency to ramble. He spent the first forty minutes of my family's initial hour visit describing how tired he was due to the massive amount of antihistamines he was taking. He also discussed, at great length, a fantastic conference he had just attended on the treatment of brain tumors. After some impatient prodding on our part, he finally dropped his little bombshell. He suggested that I might have testicular cancer that had metastasized from my testicle to my brain! Nobody had ever mentioned this possibility before. My balls immediately began to tingle with fear.

At first he said that testicular cancer was better to have than a pontine glioma, and then he said it was worse. I looked at this man and tried, through my sobbing, to get him to say everything clearly all over again. I wasn't crying about my tumor, or my future, or my testicles, or my short life. I was crying because my fate was in the hands of this poor human being with his pathetic sinuses that required too many antihistamines. I didn't want to deal with the fact that this guy was about to shoot 6,000 rads of X-rays into my fragile brain. Control, control, I felt like I was losing control. This man was too human, too susceptible to allergies, too prone to error and misjudgment. I wanted God Himself to take over my case and make sure that the radiation was aimed correctly and that I got enough of it to make certain that my tumor died. I wanted to live. But if I had to die, I wanted to do it on my own terms and certainly not at the hands of Dr. E.

Dr. E. ended his presentation with a "look at the pictures." He pointed at something on one of the CAT scans. "There's the tumor," he said confidently. He was looking at an old scan that had been interpreted as completely negative.

"Uh-h-h, Dr. E., that is supposedly a negative scan you're looking at."

"Oh well, uh, of course, I'm no radiologist and I'm gonna have THE EXPERTS looking at these things to tell me where to go with the radiation…"

It was a mind-boggling consultation. Doctors had frightened me before but this guy took the cake. My parents, friends, and I spent the entire weekend trying to figure out exactly what Dr. E. had said, what it all meant, and whether to even stay with him as the radiotherapist.

The following Monday we called Dr. C. and asked him to make sure that Dr. E. was operating with all systems intact. Dr. C. consulted with Dr. E. and got back to us. He assured us that Dr. E. was our man. Dr. C. said that the idea about testicular cancer was probably wrong—but was a good idea. We decided to go with Dr. E.

□

In an effort to validate Dr. E.'s idea about testicular cancer, I was given an ultrasound examination of my testicles. And I thought I had seen everything. A very well-dressed doctor put K-Y Jelly all over my balls and proceeded to fondle them for two hours with an optical probe. I passed this test of homophobia with flying colors. My testicles were completely normal, and I didn't have a single erection the entire time. At one point during the exam the good doctor looked down at me and kindly said that he understood how ridiculous I must be feeling. Me feel ridiculous? This poor slob had spent seven years in school in exchange for the rare privilege of fondling my balls with K-Y Jelly for two hours: who was in the more ridiculous position? The testicular ultrasound was normal. I didn't have cancer of the balls.

I used to lie on the therapy table while I was receiving my "rads" and mentally swear at the tumor, (Watch out you motherfucker, you're gonna' fry in hell you fucking-pain-in-the-ass-cancer-piece-of-shit, these rads are

gonna fry your stinking fucking asshole into SHIT!)
only to be interrupted by the silence at the end of the
treatment.

In order to keep down brain swelling from both the
tumor and the radiation therapy, I was given high doses
of an extremely powerful synthetic steroid hormone. The
steroids led to immediate and welcome relief from many
of my uncomfortable neurological problems. They also
had amazingly potent side effects. I developed a mania for
completeness. I read every article in the *Los Angeles Times*,
from every section, every day. I was as well versed in the
Polish Solidarity situation as many members of our State
Department. My long-term memory became untrust-
worthy however, and I didn't retain data well. I always felt
irritable and short tempered around other people. I lost
my sex drive. It, along with everything else in my life, was
replaced by an absolutely insatiable hunger, regardless of
how full my stomach was.

Dr. E. didn't know whether this last side effect was
physiological or psychological. He didn't know what
was going on. But he noted the same syndrome in every
patient of his who took steroids.

"Well, hell, Jim—you've got to be very careful about
that," he cautioned, "or else you'll gain fifteen pounds
before you're through here!"

I must not have been careful enough because in
the six weeks of radiation therapy I gained more than
twenty-five pounds. Normally I am a light man, with a

fighting weight of 135 pounds. I have always had a normal appetite. While on steroids I could easily pack away five full-course meals a day. I ate food like a rhinoceros, I loved every bite of everything. I thought of food between meals, during meals, during sleep, before sleep, during sex, and even while watching boxing on TV. I woke up in the morning thinking of my breakfast plans, and I went to bed at night, every night, stuffed to the point of stomach distension—with my gut stretched out from some delicious late-night snack.

I devised intricate schemes to try and keep myself from eating the wrong foods, none of which worked. The problem was that I ate whatever was put in front of me with the fervor and bliss of a hungry dog. I used to eat an ample dinner every night with my parents. Then, under the pretense of taking an after-dinner walk, I would go down to the hamburger stand near their apartment. I would quickly throw down a couple of burgers and a shake. By the time I had waddled back home, Mom would be ready with an elaborate snack! Boom! Toss in a little late-night dessert and it's only seven hours to "pre-radiation-therapy breakfast," nine hours until "post-radiation-therapy breakfast," and then lunch, dinner, more burgers, snack, breakfast, lunch, until I became one big disgusting ball of fat. I knew I had gone too far the day my sister looked at me while I was lying on my back and told me I reminded her of a beached whale.

The steroids masked many uncomfortable symptoms, but they also reinforced my feelings of being out of control of my life—feelings engendered by my developing a cancer in the first place. I lost control of my body when it gave birth to a cancer against my wishes. The process of radiation therapy provided little room for me to regain control. The steroids made the circle complete. Now I couldn't even control my appetite.

☐

The issue of self-control is critical for any person with cancer. People are able to confront the most awful situations with dignity, so long as they feel in control of their fate. Most doctors are ignorant of this simple need. In fact, they seem to have their own psychological need for control. This gets in the way of the patient's desire to regain the reins of his or her life. Unfortunately, when a doctor's needs are in conflict with those of the patient, the patient suffers.

These feelings of being out of control are further imprinted on the patient by an authoritarian system of medical care. By authoritarian, I mean a power relationship based on something other than an equal sharing of roles. I was expected to obey the doctors because they possessed superior knowledge.

Because the steroids were masking my symptoms, I never got to see if the radiation was working. My symptoms appeared to be gone. This may have temporarily made my life more comfortable, but it also deprived me of the important experience of watching my therapy work. I was never able to empirically observe the radiation therapy taking effect. I got sick and went on steroids. I seemed to be getting better, but this appearance was only a result of the drugs.

To add yet another layer of mystery, my constant efforts to find out from Dr. E. exactly when he was planning to end the therapy always led to such vague responses that I assumed the decision was still up in the air—dependent on how well I tolerated and responded to the radiation.

Then, one day after my treatment, the technicians began congratulating me on successfully completing the therapy. Nobody had bothered to tell me that this was my last day! I was only the patient, the least important part of the process. I was expendable. There would be many more patients coming through Dr. E.'s doorway. I was one of almost fifty "heads" being irradiated at that time, and I was probably not close to being the most interesting or challenging case.

It turns out that Dr. E. had simply divided my planned total radiation dosage into equal daily allotments. It would have been easy for him to have told me exactly when the therapy was going to end from the very first day it began. But telling me this might have engendered some minor feeling of control on my part, and fostering a patient's feelings that he is in control was not, at least to Dr. E., a desired element in our relationship.

The real name of the game here is "expropriation." The doctors take an already physically weakened human being and place him or her in the hospital. This bizarre environment quickly expropriates all of that person's individuality: clothes, eating habits, sleeping habits, privacy, friends, personality—everything about the patient gets swallowed up in the impersonal indecency of hospital life. After the patient is thus made captive, the medical gods swoop down from above for a few minutes each day, uttering their lofty pronouncements that carry so much import. The overtaxed central nervous system of their befuddled patient has now become mush.

The patient can no longer effectively make decisions. The doctors have a monopoly on the knowledge, and they expropriate the patient's ability to control his or her predicament. No patient can operate the technological machinery used for medical diagnosis and treatment. Knowledge, and power over himself, are the only weapons available for a very sick person to use in the fight against disease. By taking that knowledge and power out of the patient's hands, the doctors leave the patient feeling absolutely dependent.

The technicians, nurses, orderlies, patient transporters, laboratory workers, etc. are necessary for the proper delivery of health care. Often, it is the doctors who are the unnecessary factor in the equation. After more than two years of dealing with doctors, I have developed an allergic reaction to them. I now believe that if I continue to seek their advice they will ultimately kill me—kill me with their scientific rationalism, kill me with their assumption of control over my body, kill me with the sense of the authoritarian power inherent in their position.

The day that my radiation therapy ended so abruptly, I sought out Dr. E. for my "last day of therapy consultation." Dr. E. had left town for a two-week vacation and in his place was a Dr. H. I had to keep staring at Dr. H.'s name tag to remind myself that this sorry character was really a doctor. He was wearing an open-necked bowling shirt, which revealed a coffee-stained undershirt to complement his musty coffee breath. He was attempting to sprout a mustache. As he examined me, I got a good look at the pathetic crop of hairs, pimples, dingleberries, and food crumbs that had aggregated to form a weak excuse for an upper lip hair growth. I knew at once not to bring up anything too complex with this guy. I made sure that everyone had calculated correctly and that this truly was my last day of therapy. I was still ingesting steroids, and I asked how quickly I could taper off the medication. When I told him my dosage level he smiled smugly. Surely this was a simple enough question—one that he could easily answer.

"Hey, you're essentially off them now and you don't even know it! That's a homeopathic (totally inconsequential) dose. Go home and throw the rest of those pills in the toilet."

Ten hours later I was home, bleeding from both nostrils. I had a headache that felt like there were separate brain tumors on each hair follicle. A call to Dr. C. revealed that I had gone off the steroids much too abruptly and I was suffering from the resultant brain swelling. Over the next few days I gradually tapered down my steroid dosage and had no subsequent problems.

CHAPTER NINE

Round Two

DURING THE RADIATION THERAPY I MANAGED
to complete my unfinished year of medical school. The
combination of steroids and 6,000 rads to the brain had
a dulling effect on my memory, but I stumbled through
a series of final exams and I was promoted to second
year. I remember feeling a compulsive need not to miss
any school, not to fall behind, and not to get off the track
toward becoming a doctor. After all, it was the doctors who
had "saved my life" by their heroic efforts. I never gave
any serious thought to taking time off from school. I was
trying to reduce the status of my brain tumor to that of a
headache.

There were just two weeks of vacation between the
end of radiation therapy and the beginning of school. I
needed more time to assess my shattered *weltanschauung*.
I needed more time to relax. But I was a medical student. I had important classes to attend. I was determined
to unlock the mysteries of the organism so that I could
pass the knowledge on to my patients! Basically, I tried
to shrug off my lesson in mortality by burying myself in
the sterile, limited, nonthreatening seminary of medical

school. My plan was to work so hard in school that I wouldn't have any time left for cancer.

Six weeks into the academic year, I was walking down the hall when I suddenly noticed that my eye problem was back. The old double vision again. Within a few days, all of my symptoms had returned. Holy shit, when was this gonna end? Six goddamned weeks, six little motherfuckers, what the fuck did I go through all those scans for, and losing my hair, and gaining a ton of weight? Damn it, I didn't go through all that crap for a lousy, stinking six weeks.

Dr. C. felt it was highly unlikely that my tumor had grown back so quickly. He suggested that my problems, though they looked exactly like a tumor regrowth, were probably due to a swelling of my brain from the heavy load of radiation. He felt that after a few days of steroids, I would be back on my feet again. Two weeks of steroid therapy failed to do much more than reconstruct the doughnut around my waistline. I was convinced my tumor had grown back and I was going to die. I went into the hospital twice during this period. I underwent then another series of invasive, painful, medieval explorations of my brain like the one I had been subjected to the previous summer.

This time however, I added a new wrinkle to the process—morphine! Oh, sweet, sweet morphine. I told the doctors that I needed to get high to make it through each test. For the particularly awful tests I didn't mess around.

I told them they could do anything they wanted, but first they would have to put me to sleep. The good doctors were more than happy to oblige. After all, a sleeping patient is a compliant patient. Hospital-quality morphine and Demerol can make the most barbaric intrusion on one's person seem very pleasant, and the post-morphine snoozes I experienced were like nectar from the gods.

Somehow, I made it through. There were many times during these hospitalizations when I thought I was at the end of my rope. Little did I realize that the curtain was just going up on the second act of my little tragedy.

□

The confusion and lack of consensus among the doctors reached epic proportions during this phase. Someone decided that a CAT scan would show everything, so I had a CAT scan. It didn't show anything. A "contrast-enhanced" CAT scan will show it! I had that, too. It didn't show a thing. Neither did a "contrast-enhanced metrizamide" scan. I knew what was coming—the ball-buster, old faithful, a pneumoencephalogram. Air right into the brain pan. For the ten days following the test, a headache with every frown, smile, breath, sneeze, wheeze, wink, and blink. This test has generally been replaced by the less-invasive and less-painful CAT scan. In my case, it was the only test that showed the tumor. I knew that eventually they would get around to doing it again. They did.

During this week, my family and friends were receiving completely contradictory information from each doctor with whom they spoke. After one test, a neurologist came in to tell me that my scans showed changes indicating a possible tumor mass. "But that doesn't mean anything," he said, because eight weeks following radiation therapy was not enough time for my tumor to disappear. The mass that everyone was seeing was probably the original tumor, not a regrowth.

The very next morning another doctor entered my room, brimming over with good news. He said that everyone had reevaluated my scan. They now felt that yesterday's mass was probably not there. "But that doesn't mean anything," he said, because there wasn't enough detail on the scan to make accurate judgments about it. Oh, . . . yeah, sure. I was beginning to feel as if my job as a patient was to help the doctors reach some sort of consensus. I wanted to help them out. I wanted to have something very easy to diagnose. Maybe if they found out what was wrong they would stop torturing me.

The day of the dreaded "pneumo" arrived. I got jacked up on a nice dose of morphine delivered by one of my favorite nurses. I must say that, in total contradiction to my expectations, the nurses I encountered were absolutely incredible. They were warm, thoughtful, humane, and concerned. I know there are bad nurses and cruel nurses and nurses who just don't give a damn. But my experiences with nurses were great. I gave them as little trouble as possible and didn't bother them about small things. I showed them the same respect I showed my doctors. They always responded with acts of kindness and minor infringements of hospital policy that made life on the ward more bearable.

I remember talking with my brother in the hall before the test. I was zonked out of my mind. I began realizing what a wonderful fellow he was, and how deep my love for him was, and how there was nobody in the world with whom I would rather spend the last moments of my life, when all of a sudden, WHAM! The test was over and I was back in my hospital room. I saw my father's face hovering over me—it looked flushed. I began to worry about his blood pressure getting too high. He was trying to tell me that my tumor was back and that I could get chemotherapy. All I heard was "the tumor is back . . . chemotherapy . . . the tumor is back . . . the tumor . . . ," and I slipped off into a morphine-induced sleep.

My doctors all agreed that my tumor had come back. They felt that chemotherapy was now my best treatment option. All I knew was that I felt sick as a dog and the steroids weren't helping. I was ready to do anything required to stay alive, even if it meant withstanding the horrible rigors of chemotherapy. I was sent to a brand new "Comprehensive Cancer Clinic" at UCLA, where I had an appointment with a hematologist, Dr. Y.

During my hospitalization, one of my liver tests was slightly abnormal. This was probably due to laboratory error or a side effect of steroid therapy. Dr. Y. had zealously followed up on this red herring with daily finger sticks, blood tests, and finally an excruciatingly painful bone-marrow test. All of these tests proved to be completely negative.

Dr. Y. was intrigued by the fact that the type of tumor for which I was treated is mostly, although not exclusively, found in young children. He had convinced himself that I was suffering from a malady other than a pontine glioma and he was bound and determined to find the alternative problem. He wanted to test me further, at the risk of brain damage and even death. Chained as he was to the statistics indicating I was too old for my disease, Dr. Y. single-mindedly pursued other diagnoses. Had he been my primary physician, he might very well have killed me in his pursuit.

Dr. Y. kept me waiting for three hours. It is difficult to describe how slowly time passes in a medical waiting room when one is in need of critical information. Time creeps and crawls along like a slug. Ten minutes of clock time becomes an eternity. Three hours of game shows on the waiting room TV, cups of coffee, trips to the bathroom, sick people, secretaries, messengers, doctors, photocopy machine repairmen, and old copies of *Forbes* magazine. It's enough to drive you berserk.

I finally got into the examining room. The staff could not locate my chart. Another half hour went by. My chart arrived. Fifteen minutes later Dr. Y. entered. He studied my chart intently while I sat and watched him. This took ten minutes. Finally, after adjusting himself in his chair, he said, "Well I have a new theory."

Great—that's all I needed. A new theory. I was beginning to feel like my brain tumor was actually someone else's research project.

He continued, "My basic feeling is that until we biopsy the tumor, we don't have any idea of what we're dealing with." Then he started in on his plan of attack. He recommended that I have a brain biopsy immediately so he could feel secure about what "we" were dealing with. This reluctance to treat me without surgically removing tumor cells had been expressed before by many of the doctors. Dr. C. had not liked the idea of pouring 6,000 rads into my brain without a physical sample of what he was destroying. However, in discussing the desirability of a brain biopsy, Dr. C. had said that he didn't want to put me through it. "The goddamned procedure has a 50 percent mortality rate," he told me. He was not ready to take that kind of risk. Neither was I.

Dr. Y. voiced no such reservations. His plan: an immediate brain biopsy. This would confirm the diagnosis by showing the cell type of my tumor. This information would be "extremely helpful in determining the course of chemotherapy treatment." While he was on the subject, I wondered if he could possibly tell me about the different chemotherapeutic options available. Dr. Y. was happy to oblige.

"There's essentially only one drug being used for brain tumor chemotherapy—BCNU." He then went on to explain that BCNU doesn't really work anyway, and that the best result I could expect would be a 20 percent chance of response.

"By response, Dr. Y., I assume you mean cure, right?"

Wrong. By "response" he was talking about extending my life for a matter of weeks. Weeks! Weeks...weeks. Weeks, not of joyful, productive work and fulfillment of last wishes, but weeks of recovery from a brain biopsy, of pain, hair loss, no appetite, weeks of family and friends watching me wither away like a rotten piece of fruit.

As Dr. Y. rambled on, he suddenly appeared to be miles away. I felt as if I had just taken peyote. I was huge. I could see over the edge of the world. This man was in a small conference room with me, yet he looked very far away. I glanced over at my brother, who was sitting next to me on the examining table. He now seemed to be sitting about a hundred miles due west. I wondered if he understood the insanity and irrationality of the man in the room with us. Did my brother see the foolishness of that confident, overtrained, intelligent, well-meaning young man? Did my brother understand that Dr. Y. had unquestioningly swallowed an ideology that forced him into a position of utter logical confusion?

I was confident that Dr. Y.'s recommendations would fall on deaf ears. Yet when he called my other doctors, they felt that Dr. Y. was being entirely reasonable. Except for some minor reservations about the brain biopsy, they encouraged me to follow his advice.

Before I did anything, I decided to check with one more doctor, Dr. J. My best friend Joe had made a number of calls to different doctors in an effort to be my advocate and was ecstatic when I mentioned Dr. J. "All roads lead to Dr. J.," Joe said. He was impressed with the number of people who had mentioned his name— Dr. J. was "The Man" in brain chemotherapy. Dr. J. also had a reputation as an excellent brain surgeon. I hustled up to see him in San Francisco, bringing along all of my files, photos, CAT scans, X-rays, doctor's notes, etc. I was hopeful that he would give me the straight dope on what chemotherapy had to offer me.

I can't emphasize enough the difficulties a patient has in trying to consult with someone like Dr. J. Usually it's hard to schedule an emergency appointment with any doctor, no matter how famous he or she is. It is an exceptional doctor who has an appointment slot available within a reasonable period of time. Often, the simple logistics of arranging for the delivery of medical records can be Kafkaesque. These records are usually far more valuable to the consulting doctor than the patient's body. The process of getting them delivered to a doctor brings the patient up against the stone wall of hospital rules and regulations concerning the release of medical information. The patient just wants the records sent. The hospital wants to follow the rules and avoid getting sued. The workers in medical records don't give a damn about anything except staying within the confines of their jobs. Nobody in charge gives a shit.

Compounding these problems is the fact that the patient starts out in a compromised position. He or she is lucky indeed to have enough energy and tolerance to take care of this business. The frustration of the process further reinforces a patient's dependence on the goodwill of others. We have a medical system with the technology to produce an artificial heart. Soon we will be able to design pocket computers that can stimulate the muscles of paraplegics, allowing them to walk. We can replace skin, limbs, and most of the major organs—but we don't have a workable system of mailing records from one doctor to another! The University of California at Los Angeles has no protocol established for sending medical records to the University of California, San Francisco!

With all of this in mind, I was relieved to find that Dr. J.'s office had received my records. My parents, my friend Laurie, and I sat around for the now obligatory two-hour wait. We were finally ushered into the inner sanctum of the good doctor.

I had experienced all kinds of bizarre things in doctor's offices, but I was ill-prepared for Dr. J.'s style. As we entered his office, he was sitting behind his desk, poring over all of the medical forms and scans that we had worked so diligently to provide. He barely acknowledged our presence in the room. We spent the first twenty minutes of the appointment watching him study my voluminous chart. Every once in a while he would write something down or ask me a question. "How much radiation did you receive?" Ten minutes of silence. "What cell type do they think your tumor is composed of?" Five more minutes of deadly silence.

After an unbearable period of this, Dr. J. hit us with his best shot. He told us that he couldn't tell much of anything from my records. He couldn't tell where my tumor was located, whether or not it was inside my brain, whether or not it was a recurrence. In short, he couldn't say anything. He refused to answer any questions about the potential of chemotherapy. His recommendation? Go back home to Los Angeles, get plenty of rest, get a "good" CAT scan, and, hopefully, all of my problems would turn out to be a delayed radiation reaction.

I remember the numb state of shock that I immediately went into. In the course of five minutes, Dr. J. the world-renowned expert, had completely contradicted six months of opinions I had received from the doctors in Los Angeles. These doctors had all been confident about the location and type of my brain tumor. In fact, they had been self assured enough to pour 6,000 rads into my head on the basis of the pictures that this maniac was now calling worthless. "Get another CAT scan." I had already gotten at least ten of the motherfuckers! What would one more show? I was absolutely furious. I felt destined to spend the rest of my pathetic life trying to get this ever-expanding bunch of asshole doctors to agree on something. Anything! Maybe if the doctors reached a consensus of opinion I could adjust to whatever it was and go on to live my life.

After this appointment with Dr. J., I sat down in the hospital lobby with my folks. Their faces kept coming in and out of my field of view. I knew they were saying encouraging things, positive things designed to bolster my flagging spirits. After a while we went out to a restaurant where I ordered clam chowder. It tasted like death. I noticed the Monday night football game on the TV above the bar. I wasn't watching the players with my usual analytic enthusiasm. I was staring autistically at the green football field, and the white of the chalk marks, and the uniforms of the referees. I wondered if Dr. J. was watching the game at home. I went back to the table and excused myself to go out to the car. I lay in the back seat and stared out at the black sky and the stars. My mind had been deep-fried by my consultation with Dr. J., and now I was struggling to pull the pieces back together.

My parents dropped Laurie and me off at the airport. As we waited for our flight, I called Joe for advice.

A black airport janitor overheard my end of the conversation and came up to me after it was over. Was I Jewish? When I answered yes, he assured me that his whole church would be praying for me. I shouldn't worry because Jesus would heal me. I was in such a frazzled state of mind that I almost believed him. I bought $50,000 worth of flight insurance for $1.50. During the plane ride home, I prayed that the plane would crash and I would be the only passenger killed. My family would get the money and live happily ever after. To my great disappointment, we touched down safely in L.A.

I returned home as depressed as I've ever been. My mind was filled with images of doctors, CAT scans, needles, operating rooms, hospitals, airplanes crashing...what did it all mean? I must have messed up somewhere; all of it was simply too absurd and I was losing my ability to cope.

A few days later I enlisted the help of a friend. He dragged my ass to a private CAT scanning office where I received scan number eleven. I did it even though I was convinced that it was going to be as useless as the previous ten. My friend dropped me off at home afterward. I had just settled into bed for a nap when I received a call from the secretary at the CAT scan office. She told me they had screwed up on my scan and asked if I would please come back tomorrow to try again. I agreed and hung up the phone. Sure, I'd come back. Sure, I'd be glad to do the scan one more time. I love radioactive iodine.

I began to cry. I was crying because it was all too unfair
and absurd and I wasn't cut out for any of this. I should
have been out hitting softballs, and going to Mexico,
and bird-dogging women, and jogging, and advancing
through school, and laughing—where was the humor in
all of this? The humor thus far had been black and tragic.
But the best was yet to come.

CHAPTER TEN

Living with Cancer

I MADE A SPONTANEOUS RECOVERY FROM MY neurological problems. The doctors assumed that the most recent episode had been caused by post-radiation brain swelling. I made my first compromise to cancer: I wore an eye patch over my right eye to prevent the double vision which otherwise occurred. I knew that this double vision was a permanent result of brain damage due to radiation. The eye patch would be my badge of courage, a symbol of my struggle against cancer. Other than that problem, all of my neurologic symptoms completely cleared up.

I was free. I had survived the tumor and the treatment. Cancer no longer loomed over my fragile life like a sword, threatening to cut it short. Life-so-sweet! I could now take a deep breath of fresh air without feeling that it might be my last. I could go to sleep knowing that I would wake up to greet a new day. I was going to read more front pages, see more Dodger games, go back to school, have children, be a famous cancer epidemiologist, watch the rain outside my window. . . . I could live like a normal human being without that tight, cold feeling in the pit of my stomach—the fear of death.

I experienced almost six months of moderately good health. I had free time (I had taken a year off from medical school) and I spent it reading, swimming, and relaxing. I made ends meet by working on a couple of motion pictures that friends of mine were making. I joined a support group composed solely of people with cancer. We all became warm friends as we shared the special horrors of having this disease. I started going to a psychiatrist in an attempt to pull together the shattered pieces of my worldview. He was exceptionally helpful. He directed me to confront the important issues of anger, control, and dependence—issues which are critical to anyone with cancer.

I regained about 90 percent of my previous state of good health. I even jogged a couple of miles on two different occasions. The highlight of my recovery was a camping trip to the desert with friends. We capped off the last day of the trip with a strenuous five-mile hike. I handled it with ease. I was going to make it! I was going to beat a tumor—not just any tumor but a malignant brain tumor! Each day crackled with an electricity, a freedom.

There were ominous signs, however. One day I was talking on the phone, making an appointment for a patient at the Free Clinic. All of a sudden, I noticed that I was slurring words every once in a while. A few weeks later I noticed a tremor occurring in my left hand. My left leg began to act unreliably as well. I would mention all of these things to Dr. C. during our monthly consultations. He kept reassuring me that my problems were most likely due to radiation damage. I would leave his office feeling like I must be the most neurotic patient Dr. C. had ever seen. Here I was, scared to death over a little radiation damage. I would also leave his office with the familiar feeling of not having been attended to. This was the same feeling that I was left with after almost every appointment with a doctor. I felt as if my doctors and I were speaking different languages. There must have been something wrong with me...something wrong with my mind.

There *was* something wrong with my mind. I was suffering from a recurrence of my brain tumor. One day I limped into Dr. C.'s office for my regularly scheduled appointment. I told him I was freaking out. Everything was getting inexorably and inexplicably worse. I told him that I was sure my problems stemmed from a regrowth of the tumor, and I didn't want to leave his goddam office one more time feeling like I was walking around with a brain tumor that my own doctor had missed. He said that I "looked too healthy to have a brain tumor," but if it would put me at ease he would arrange for CAT scan number thirteen. At this point, my patience was wearing thin. I was tired of the whole scene: CAT scans, medical assessments my grandmother could have made, and living the half-life of a cancer patient.

CAT scan number thirteen was the same as the previous twelve, except for one variation. The machine was the newest model available, and the hospital didn't have time to install it in its permanent place. They were keeping it in a mobile home out in the parking lot. Further reinforcing my feeling of alienation was the staff: the same group of unfortunates who had barbecued me on so many previous occasions. They were waiting for me inside of that awful trailer. What a motley crew.

"Have you ever had radioactive iodine before?" Nurse Dogface asked.

(Oh, come on lady, you personally gave me this shit at least five times before!) "Yes."

"Well then, you know what to expect, don't you?" she asked as though I were a two-year-old.

"Yeah, well, uh, I'd like to ask you to please put the stuff in slowly. Otherwise I get kinda....

"Oh, sure," she said vacantly, but the expression on her face said, "SORRY BUDDY. THERE'S ONE SPEED AND ONE SPEED ONLY ON THIS BOAT, AND THAT'S FULL SPEED AHEAD!"

So of course she gave me the stuff too quickly and I got sick to my stomach. As I lay on the table during that test, I made a vow never to undergo such indignities again. I never have.

I would like to report that the scan was negative and that I recovered completely, became the heavyweight champion of the world, and went on to market prosthetic devices for brain-damaged people...but that's not quite the way it turned out. The scan was positive—my tumor had grown back. I was now squarely facing what all of my cancer books called "the deepest fear of every cancer patient: recurrence."

Dr. C. recommended that I go see a new guy, Dr. F. Dr. F. was in charge of a gamma radiation machine. It sounded like a wonderful invention. Only one treatment was necessary. The whole thing lasted forty-five minutes. There was no hair loss and no brain damage outside of the irradiated zone. GIVE IT TO ME YOU MANIACS BECAUSE I WANT TO LIVE!

Dr. F. tried to be reassuring. There were only two sets of obstacles to my receiving the gamma radiation. The first set: my tumor might be too large, in the wrong place, or the wrong kind of tumor. Okay, what else? The second set sounded more odious. Gamma radiation had previously only been tested on dogs. We would have to get special written dispensation from the State in order to use the machine on me. I didn't look forward to becoming human specimen numero uno. It didn't appear to me that the doctors were all that competent with the more familiar therapeutic techniques in which they were well practiced. I could only imagine the horrible mistakes these clowns might make with this new toy, using my battered pincushion of a body as their first test site.

Dr. F. made two revealing errors as our consultation came to an end: he became what seemed like the five-hundredth doctor to tell me "we'll find the solution to your problem," and he admonished me to "have faith."

Have faith. Faith in what? Silly-ass shitbag doctors who probably didn't know the first thing about healing (or having) a brain tumor? Faith in God? If there was a God in the universe, I'm sure He had more pressing items on his agenda than my little tumor. I had about as much faith in God as I had in the Chicago Cubs winning the World Series.

There's a wise old gambling adage that says "don't throw good money after bad." Well, in terms of my chances of living out the year, I was beginning to have the odor of a real longshot. I began to wonder if it was worthwhile investing any more energy in the pursuit of a cure. To ease my mind during what Dr. F. hoped would only be a two-week wait, I took a vacation. My first stop was Las Vegas where I proceeded to drop eighty dollars. I also had to deal with all of the jaded service workers there who assumed that I was drunk because I walked and talked funny. My next stop, Kino Bay, Mexico, was much more pleasant. I enjoyed ten relaxing days on the beach—reading, swimming, and playing gin rummy with my friend.

Dr. F.'s two-week wait turned out to be a three-week wait. After a great deal of pestering on my part, he finally told me that my tumor was too large, the wrong type, and in the wrong location to be treated on the machine in Los Angeles. However, if I was willing to travel, there was another gamma machine in Stockholm, Sweden. The Swedes had acquired more experience with it than anybody in the United States. In fact, they were the only other people in the world with a gamma radiation machine. Dr. F. felt sure that they would accept me as a patient. Much to my amazement, he had not yet sent off my medical records to the Swedish doctors! Why was he moving so slowly? He was a doctor, wasn't he? He was paid to use his head, wasn't he? Was this small bit of foresight on his part too much to expect?

The lethargy of my doctors was a consistent problem I encountered. I can't count the number of times I came up against the insufferable, boorish, plodding, methodical, linear slowness of their approaches. The race may not always belong to the swift, but the sluggishness of the doctors stood in sharp contrast to the nonstop progression of my cancer. My tumor was not in the mood to wait for Dr. F. to get off his duff. My doctors were in danger of being lapped by my cancer.

I tried to impress upon Dr. F. that my brain was being shredded at a prodigious rate, and it would be nice to get some therapy while there was still a little gray matter worth saving. He agreed that time was "of the essence" and he hoped we'd have an answer "within the week." A week went by with no response from Sweden. Two weeks crept by at an agonizingly slow pace. No response. Dr. F. was getting more and more evasive and vague each time I spoke to him on the phone.

At the end of the third week of waiting, I called Dr. F. "Listen Dr. F., I have really had enough of this bullshit.

We live in the twentieth century, right? And Sweden has entered the Industrial Age? We have telephones and they have telephones. SO WHY DON'T YOU GIVE THEM A PHONE CALL AND PUT ME OUT OF MY MISERY? Dr. F. called them immediately.

Of course the doctors in Sweden would be glad to do my treatment free of charge and I went over there and they cured me with one forty-five minute treatment and now I'm a successful carpet salesman...whoops! This is supposed to be nonfiction...and, of course, they said that my tumor was too large, the wrong cell type, and in the wrong location for me to be eligible for treatment. This was the exact same thing I had been told by the doctors in this country. Dr. F. called me with the bad news and mumbled something about how sorry he was that he couldn't help me. As he spoke, I could hear him light up and take a drag on a cigarette. I felt a strange euphoria. I realized how happy I was that I no longer had any traditional medical options left. I was free of the bumbling, lethargic, self-important, cigarette smoking, overworked, over-trained zealots of modern medicine. These people were bound and determined to get me to die in a hospital bed or on an operating room table.

No way, Baby! It was now obvious that I would die soon, but I was going to have the choice of where it would happen. I would rather it happen in the toilet at Dodger Stadium than in the finest of hospital suites. Other people may have different needs. A few people from my cancer support group have died this year. A couple of them died at home, one checked into a hospital, and three went on vacation for the big event. Personally, if my illness had allowed, I would have hit the road. Unfortunately, I can no longer walk, talk, or drive. My neurological problems force me to go with my second choice: at home. Just don't put me back in that hospital! The only way I would go back there is over my dead body, and they don't want patients who are already dead. They want you when you're nearly dead, while you're still alive enough to stick with needles. You've got to be testable, and slightly warm.

Dr. F. concluded his maudlin little speech with an injunction to get a consultation with the chemo man, Dr. L. I had no objection to this. Once again, I went through the song and dance of getting my records sent to him. Wisely, I decided to call him before I spent the time and energy necessary to go up to San Francisco and see him. I called him every day for a week before he finally left a message for me with his secretary. His note said the same things that had wigged me out so completely the first time I had seen him. My scan wasn't clear enough for him to make any judgments about my tumor. If I wanted to check into the hospital in San Francisco for a week, he would arrange for better scans. These would allow him to make decisions about my case. . . .

The total absurdity of the medical doctors was once again becoming frightfully apparent. The CAT scan, which was so inadequate for Dr. L. was, in the words of Dr. F., "the best that money can buy...state of the art...the best in the world...the newest-generation machine." According to Dr. F., my scan "showed my tumor quite clearly." Dr. L. found the same picture inadequate and would make no judgment about treatment based on it. By the time these cowboys got together about anything important, I would be six feet under, my brain the consistency of Jell-O.

For curiosity's sake, I decided to go to UCLA's Biomedical Library and check out some information on my own. It turned out that Dr. L. had written the seminal work on brain tumor chemotherapy. He had done some pioneering research in this field. A couple of hours with his book answered all of the questions that he had been so reticent about in person. The upshot of his book was that chemotherapy simply doesn't work for the treatment of brain tumors. I found the case history of one poor man who had managed to stumble through eighteen weeks of BCNU treatment. This was the most promising story I could dig up. Eighteen fun-filled weeks of lassitude, hair loss, vein destruction—in short, eighteen weeks of medically sanctioned hell.

I'm not as scared of dying as I am of dying around a bunch of doctors. And I don't consider eighteen weeks to be "life extension." Eighteen thin little weeks. Eighteen more weeks of cancer. Eighteen cancerous weeks. That was the information that Dr. L. was holding back. That was the little nugget of gold lying at the end of my rainbow if I acted like a good cancer patient and went to San Francisco and let Dr. L. and his crew perform their horror show on my body.

I vividly remember one afternoon of reading at the UCLA Biomedical Library. I was sitting by the windows on the eighth floor. I had been reading some extremely depressing statistics about the short life spans of people afflicted with brain tumors. I looked outside just as dusk began to fall. I felt as if blinders were being lifted from my eyes, and I was seeing the world for the first time. It was crystal clear outside. Everything looked brittle. I was afraid that it all might shatter into a million pieces... the big trees being rustled by the late afternoon wind, the large group of bicycles locked up in rows, the line of newspaper machines, empty now but ready for another day of spitting out news. Once in a while, a group of medical students would stroll by, some from my class. We're in different worlds now. There was so much more than just glass and space between us. I had crossed over into a strange land filled with tumors, prognoses, diagnoses, radiation, chemotherapy, recurrences, regrowths, remissions, and response rates. The kids I watched through the window thought they were learning all about these things, but I knew they weren't. They would know the meaning of "spontaneous remission" as well as I do, but their hearts would never skip a beat upon hearing those words. They wouldn't have to alter their diets, or deal with a paralyzed limb, or be unable to speak clearly, or feel compelled to pray to a god they didn't believe in. They were not mature and they were not free. But they sure were healthy, and I was jealous.

The medical students were laughing. They were carrying enormous notebooks in their backpacks. One group stopped to talk to each other near the bicycle racks. I could see them clearly through the library window. They were probably discussing tests, or teachers, or textbooks. I felt so far away from them. The thick window glass prevented me from hearing any sounds. They went on talking and laughing. What did I expect? They were clearly in another world. We were separated by a huge gap, by a plate of window glass, by a small tumor. Something deep inside told me that I would never return to medical school.

I made one more call to Dr. F. I told him about what I had read. I said that my dealings with the doctors were not the kind of experiences I would care to repeat. I informed him that I was going to seek out alternative therapeutic modalities. I don't think he approved of my ideas. He told me that, as a medical student, I was a "member of the club." He was pretty sure he could talk somebody into giving me more radiation therapy, even though I had already been given the maximum dose. I politely declined his offer.

CHAPTER ELEVEN

The Health Farm

In a last-ditch effort to salvage my battered life, I checked into a "health farm." This place offered a program of nutritional therapy for cancer and other life-threatening diseases. There were patients from vastly different walks of life, in all kinds of physical conditions. Some were athletic, while others were barely warm. I fit nicely into the second category.

My steadfast significant other, Laurie, kindly drove down with me to La Jolla to share my last weekend before I entered the farm. We enjoyed a wonderful two days of hedonism. We ate like pigs: ice cream by the quart, deli lunches, steak dinners—all of the food I was soon to give up.

After this beautiful weekend of fun and sun, I had little desire to graze the strict dietary pastures of a health farm. I knew that there would be other terminally ill patients at the farm, many with cancer. However, I felt as if my neurological symptoms would make me stand out like a leper. By this time I walked with the aid of a cane, and my version of walking was a bizarre parody of the real thing. I was terribly self-conscious about my severely slurred speech.

Upon our arrival at the farm, Laurie and I were escorted to my room by a cheerful gnome of a man who greeted us with an enthusiastic, "All is possible in the Mind of the Divine!" I told him I hoped something could be arranged for my mind, because that's where the tumor was. He didn't appreciate my joke and directed the rest of his attention exclusively to Laurie.

He told her of his experiences with intolerable pain and double vision. He didn't know the name of his disease or its cause. Nutritional therapy had done the trick after all of his doctors failed. I felt that this guy was completely nuts, but I was heartened by his critique of the medical profession. I had come to the conclusion that doctors were incapable of helping me. I was willing to listen to anyone who advocated alternatives to their techniques. After our host departed, Laurie noted that the farm's nutritional program hadn't done much for his teeth. He had the funkiest, greenest set of choppers I'd ever seen.

Laurie helped me unpack before she took off. I settled back comfortably in my bed for a short nap. I couldn't help but notice the stark simplicity of my new room and the similarity it had to a minimum security prison facility. Block DZ, Room 3, Tier One, Bed A, lower bunk, Health Farmer Slotnick reporting for sprout class, Suh! As I drifted off to sleep I began to wonder what I should do about the steroids. Dr. F. had recommended taking them during my vacation so that I would remain "comfortable." There was little that was comfortable about taking steroids. I ate enough food to fuel a good-sized diesel engine. I could limit myself to four large meals a day, but this took all of my willpower. I knew that regular fasting was going to be an important part of my new regimen. I had also been told that nutritional therapy would not work unless I discontinued my steroids. In anticipation of the health farm's program, I had lowered my dosage considerably. I vowed to kick the 'roids cold turkey the next day. Off to sleep I went.

I was jarred awake by the sound of a bullhorn from out on the patio. The tour had started! I dressed as quickly as possible and stumbled out to join the group. We saw the health farm's amply stocked supply rooms of wheatgrass, the juice of which is the staple of the program's restricted diet. Wheatgrass grows from a wheat seed. When sprouted, harvested, and juiced it can be used orally, anally, as a poultice, a soap, or a shampoo. I was hoping that it would work as a blood and tissue detoxifier and help me cure myself of cancer.

We saw the impressive organic garden, toured the health farm grounds, and listened to our enthusiastic tour guide. He was a cheerful, very blond, very Californian "seed-head." He knew everything there was to know about organic gardening, composting, fertilizing, and sprouting. He assured us that we would be happy at the farm. Good things happened here; there was good food and good vibes. I was surrounded by people of all ages, some of whom were extremely sick, even terminally ill.

Apparently, they left feeling much better. All of this was fine by me. I was feeling so terminal that I hadn't even bothered to put a bet down on the Dodgers making it to the World Series.

During the tour I started to chat with a nice, middle-aged black lady named Nancy. She told me she was a psychic healer, and I should let her put her hands on my head as much as possible. She asked if I was Jewish, and then she told me all about her son. He had been in a terrible car accident. The doctors had given up on him and predicted he would be a vegetable for the rest of his life. Nancy had worked with her son daily for more than a year, using physical and nutritional therapy. Now he was back on the job. She thought that the doctors who had originally treated her son were overeducated fools. I agreed with her wholeheartedly.

Our castigation of the medical profession was reinforced by the revival-tent atmosphere of the lecture we then attended. All of the other visitors to the farm were there. Cancer was curable, insisted the vibrant, healthy-looking speaker. She had cured herself of breast cancer by doing two things: "I stopped seeing my doctors and I started eating properly. I immediately began to get better." Her words sent a chill down my spine. I was already convinced that my doctors were conspiring to kill me. Leaving them behind would cause me no pain. I was ready to eat anything if it would help me get well: fly carcasses, metal shavings, camel dung—bring it to me!

I'd eat it all and beg for more! Just help me get rid of this damn tumor!

I had a profound feeling that I was in the right place. Perhaps there was a rationale behind the nutritional therapy. The speaker's experience had convinced her that proper nutrition would help the body cure itself of cancer. She had been a research consultant for a well-known American university. Scientists there had run experiments in an attempt to compare the results of nutritional therapies for cancer to the standard medical modalities. The study was stopped when preliminary results indicated that nutritional therapies were more effective than traditional techniques (chemotherapy, radiation, surgery). The early data indicated that an approach to cancer treatment based upon nutrition was the only thing that worked at all. The speaker was followed to the podium by her husband. He gave a synopsis of his wife's recovery and affirmed everything she had said. The doctors had written her off as terminally ill. She had survived due to a program of drastic nutritional intervention.

I felt very good. Maybe I could beat this tumor. Without the tumor I could return to medical school. After graduation, I'd have a long and fruitful career fighting the unnecessary death and disease spawned by the medical establishment. Hope surged into my heart, and I realized how long I had been without it. I had spent the last two years under a dark cloud—staring eyeball to eyeball with cancer death. This was not the proper way for anyone to live. It was as though I was being forced to piss away all of my assets in Vegas, playing games that were rigged against me from the start. The longer I played, the more I lost, and the more I lost, the more difficult it became to continue. I had almost given up hope.

My first meal on the farm was a wonderful experience. I was still under the influence of steroids, and cow poop would have tasted great. The farm's food was delicious and I ate it with gusto, even though I couldn't identify half of the stuff on my plate. The food looked like grass and smelled healthy. After this meal, I didn't feel hungry. It was the first time that a single meal had been filling to me since I began taking steroids. I didn't crave seconds or dessert! This part of the program was going to be a piece of cake—or rather, a slice of cucumber.

After dinner we were treated to an orientation speech by the director. She was authoritarian, dogmatic, tough, and basically unlikeable. Her attitude about what went on at the farm was fascistic. We were not to discuss our illnesses with the staff or other guests. This was a hard and fast rule. It struck me as unnecessary and potentially harmful. I had spent the past nine months as an active member of a cancer support group, in which everyone shared their experiences with the disease. I had found this to be tremendously helpful.

The director's view was typically "Californian." My home state fertilizes the growth of many groups whose philosophy is based on the creative power of individual consciousness. The underlying rationale behind prohibiting discussion of health problems was that "recognition" of a problem "gives the problem a basis in reality." The patient gives the disease its credibility, indeed its very existence. This is a peculiarly Hegelian concept: consciousness determines being. This notion created a conflict for me. After all, Karl Marx was my main man! Hadn't he turned Hegel on his head and proposed that being determines consciousness? Our tumors had created our need to talk about our health problems, and not the other way around. How was I going to change my thought patterns, assumptions, and ideas in time to cure my tumor? Was there a special cure for Marxists?

While in theory the director's ruling was bothersome, in practice, it was widely disobeyed. Most of us were hungry to share our feelings with others who were experiencing the same problems. I rationalized my disobedience fiscally. After all, I was the one paying the bill, and I would decide what I talked about, and to whom.

The most disturbing aspect of the director's talk was her atomistic approach to our health problems. When she looked at us she saw a bunch of individuals who had been afflicted with cancer. I looked at the same people and saw a group of luckless victims of a preventable disease. The director's philosophy embodied the notion that we, as individuals, played a part in the development of our cancers. Therefore, we each had the responsibility to take care of our own problems. Patient, heal thyself.

I certainly accepted the latter half of her equation. A person with cancer had better prepare for a long, lonely battle. Most tumors love to grow, grow, grow! Other people can help out and make life easier for the cancer victim, but there isn't a doctor, therapist, herbalist, healer, friend, lover, lawyer, or parent who can remove someone's cancer. Dealing with my tumor is my responsibility. What I could not accept was the director's assertion that we were personally responsible for the initiation of our disease. At an early stage of my illness, I felt terribly guilty about my tumor. I felt that I was a horrible person, dragging my family and friends through this awful disease with me. The guilt and shame were overwhelming until I talked about it with a friend of mine who is a counselor for rape victims. She said that I sounded exactly like her clients. I was blaming myself for an event that was completely out of my control.

I pondered the director's speech for a while and then decided not to dwell on it. I figured that I was at the farm for nutritional therapy, not for a debate on the politics of cancer. My participation in that debate would come only after I had rid myself of the disease. I went to sleep excited about the next day and the beginning of my final round with this tumor.

My first week at the health farm was hellish, both physically and psychologically. I took myself off of the steroid medication abruptly. As a result, I suffered the now familiar headache and lethargy. I also experienced a gradual resumption of the neurological symptoms that the steroids had masked. My speech became slurred and my voice almost inaudible. My walking, which wasn't too good to begin with, worsened perceptibly. Nystagmus, an uncontrollable oscillation of my eyeballs, returned. My energy level dropped to a point where sitting up in a chair became hard work. It also became difficult for me to swallow, and I choked constantly during meals. I couldn't open my mouth more than a fraction of an inch and chewing became a struggle. I was a mess, but I managed to stumble through the program.

The food at the health farm was plentiful, but it quickly became unattractive to me. I stuck religiously to the strict diet, but I craved fresh fruit, which seemed to be in short supply. Actually, fruit was served every morning, but it was always spelled W-A-T-E-R-M-E-L-O-N. I've always loved the stuff, but after seven straight watermelon breakfasts I was ready to swim the Amazon for a fresh mango or a ripe banana.

My first week at the health farm required a three-day fast. I turned this into a three-and-a-half-day fast by vomiting up an evening meal in the presence of my first roommate and his wife. I had just started to get to know them. They had impressed me as having the collective intelligence of a turnip, but the wife turned out to be a nurse, and they both were warm, wonderful folks. They picked me off the floor, cleaned me up, and put me to bed. They also advised me not to drink the wheatgrass juice as close to a meal as I had.

The effects of the fast hit me gradually over the first few days. I got weak and lost weight. I would end up losing almost twenty pounds in my first week at the health farm—dropping into the featherweight division at a lean, mean 124 pounds. After two weeks down on the farm, I looked like a candidate for the 1982 anorexia nervosa poster boy competition. Compounding the emaciated appearance of my body was a moderate degree of muscle atrophy of my left arm and leg. The left side of my body was 90 percent paralyzed. Just like my pathology book says, "Lack of use leads to muscle atrophy." Well, I guess doctors had to be right once in a while.

In addition to the physical torture and disability I was experiencing, I was forced to make some tough psychological adjustments. By nature, I am a private person. I enjoy being alone. Here I was, stuck in a tiny room with strangers (emphasis on the strange). I was spending hours each day in the bathroom giving myself enemas while my roommates were right outside the door playing Parcheesi. I was one of the few people at the health farm with a serious illness and no personal attendant, but that was the way I wanted it. I had to do this alone. There was nobody else in the world who could take on my nausea, my headaches, or my tumor. I was the one who had to square off against cancer and face the loneliness, despair, and futility. No one else could eat the bland, crappy diet, or stick tubes up their ass, or drink the wheatgrass juice for me. If I wanted to enjoy life much longer, I would have to complete this nutty therapy.

□

During my first week I struck up a conversation with a woman who had completed her third week at the health farm. Was she happy with the results of her stay? Well, her problem had been cured but she had hated every minute of it. I appreciated her honesty. Could she be more specific? Well, she couldn't stand the dormitory-style rooms, the classes, the food, her room-mates, the staff, or the wheatgrass juice. She also found it psychologically distressing to do the enemas. I was still excited by what she had said. The word "cure" always sparked my interest. I didn't give a damn what I would be forced to endure over the next three weeks. I was ready for anything: enemas, colonics, even bestiality...if it would only lead me closer to that magic word. Just give me a piece of that cure-pie, just one little bite. I'm so hungry it feels like I haven't eaten in years. Please, just give me a little taste of "cure."

And what was the problem that led this woman to travel to the health farm for three weeks? Multiple scle-rosis? Not exactly. Cancer? Myasthenia gravis? No. Try acne. Acne...acne! Oh my God; this lady had jammed enema tubes up her ass for three weeks and had cured herself of acne! Wasn't that some evil shit for me to be listening to! I just stared at her acne-free face and thought about how I would happily jam baseball bats up my ass for three weeks if it would only lead me to a cure.

There was one factor unifying the disparate personalities at the farm, which was a major source of irritation to me. Everyone there talked constantly about God. He was going to help us all if we just had enough faith. Screw the doctors; we had Jesus on our side. We didn't need any medicine. We didn't need any therapy. All we had to do was get down on our knees and ask J. C. to come into our hearts. Zap! We'd be cured by God's glory, the natural way. The whole thing would only take a few seconds ... This was precisely the kind of drivel that I didn't want to hear. If my cure was in any way dependent upon the strength of my belief in God, then I might as well be eating dog food for all the good my diet was going to do.

"Just believe, and God will help you.... Just have faith because He can cure anything and everything.... All you've got to do is open up your heart.... My grandmother is ninety-five years old and never has to see a doctor 'cause she's got faith in our Lord."

I had many people lay hands on my head. I never felt anything when they did it. When I reported this lack of response to my "healer," the inevitable reply was that I "definitely was going to be healed in the future and that I shouldn't expect miracles overnight. Be patient with the Lord and He'll reward you...." After a few days of these experiences, I got tired of hearing about the Lord. I took one of the Jesus freaks aside. I told her that I liked her and wanted to be friends, but right now I didn't care to hear about Jesus from her or any of her family members. She kept her distance from me after that. She was probably convinced that I was a Jewish agent of the devil, placed on earth to test her resolve. Further discussion with me could only lead to trouble, nightmares, a decline in her physical condition—perhaps even an illegitimate and diabolical child!!! Meanwhile, I was left wondering if there was any room on the "miracle cure list" for an agnostic such as myself.

I can accept a point of view that says there must be a supreme being or force that created the world. I certainly cannot explain how everything got here, or what the source of the universe is, or why anything exists in the first place. If somebody wants to call the original creative force "God" or "Jesus" or whatever, that's perfectly fine with me. I can actually believe in a God of sorts. My version of God is more akin to Einstein's notion of a scientifically verifiable, rational force unifying all of the energies of the universe. But God has never been a particularly relevant or important issue in my life. Just because I now have cancer, I fail to see why God should suddenly become pertinent. Logically, I assume that my personal situation is either totally preordained by a rational God, or that I am a free agent living in a universe of free agents, and I will rise or fall on the strength of my own actions. Either God is totally in control of my cancer from beginning to end, or I can play a part in my illness. I choose to believe the latter because I find it a more comforting point of view. I mean, if God is in control of everything then He can cure me, right? But that also means that He was in control of me getting the tumor in the first place! What kind of God would make me go through all of this crap? I stand by my conception of God as a powerful, but disinterested third party.

I finally realized that the importance of God in the lives of the people at the farm was understandable in its own way. Many of these people were dealing with chronic, debilitating, life-threatening illnesses. Here they were, at a nutrition institute, seeking out an alternative form of therapy. For many of these people, including myself, there was nothing medical doctors could do to help. The doctors had given up on us, and in their infinite wisdom had pronounced us "terminally ill." Some doctors had even gone to the trouble of giving us a nice, neat time frame in which to validate their opinions.

I didn't trust my doctors to predict my death with any greater accuracy than they had displayed in other aspects of my case. I didn't even bother to ask for their silly speculations on this subject. Any doctor who thinks he or she can predict death accurately is a fool who should be strung up by the stethoscope and drummed out of the profession. The people at the health farm with serious illnesses had spent years dealing with the medical profession, making gods of their doctors. Now, when their doctors had failed them and their backs were against the wall, they made a doctor out of God.

One day, I was sitting in the health farm living room, reading my copy of *The Ring* magazine. I had read most of the articles two or three times. There was no newspaper delivery at the farm. Along with an occasional phone call or letter, this dog-eared journal was my only contact with the outside world. A. K. came and sat down beside me. He was fifty-five, very healthy, with an excellent build. He knew a lot about boxing. I liked him, and we started to talk. He told me that he, too, was a socialist. Now I really liked him! Anybody who appreciated the beauty of boxing and the subtleties of Marxism couldn't be all bad.

A few days later A. K. tried to play a trick on me. We were standing next to each other in the "prayer circle," which was organized before every meal. Although the health farm was ostensibly nonsectarian, this was an important part of the daily routine. Both A. K. and I hated its religious overtones. We participated in it as a concession to the feelings of our fellow health farmers.

Following the prayer, A. K. made an announcement: "Jim has some feelings he wants to share." I did? It was news to me. I was in a state of shock. Rather than let the old pinko embarrass me, I decided to wing it and hopefully say something cogent. I told everyone how much I liked being at the health farm and how all of the people there were so friendly and helpful. The food was great, the staff was great, the rooms were great, the health farm was great. I concluded with the famous dictum that I felt summed up my experience at the health farm: "From each according to his abilities, to each according to his needs."

Well, the health farmers must have been closet Marxists! They loved the quote. There was hardly a dry eye in the house. A. K. was laughing his ass off, ladies with cancer were tearfully hugging me, and business cards were flying in my direction from all sides. One belonged to a guy who owned a string of motels across Texas. Only nonsmokers could stay in them. I could now stay in them free of charge, any time I wanted. I wasn't a smoker, was I? No, I wasn't a smoker. I was something worse than that. I was a raving, born again Jewish Communist bent on destroying the tumor that was oppressing his brain. I was going to have to do it without God's help.

My second week at the farm was much better than the first. The Jesus freaks stayed away from me. A. K. turned out to be a chess player, and this gave me something to occupy my time. A fellow health farmer drove me into town where I bought a new *The Ring* and a *Los Angeles Times*. The English were moving toward the Falklands, Israel was moving into Lebanon, and the Dodgers were moving from first to second place in the National League West, losing game after game with frightening regularity. I decided to head home. I was convinced that I could now beat this tumor. Wheatgrass juice up the bunghole—that was the trick. Who needed doctors? I had my enema bag, my positive mental attitude, my mental imagery tape. . . . I was going to kick the hell out of my tumor.

CHAPTER TWELVE

On Cancer and Death

I cried so much just like a child that's lost its toy
Maybe baby, you think these tears I cry are tears of joy
A child can cry so much until you do everything they say
But unlike a child my tears don't help me to get my way
Ain't that peculiar
Peculiar as can be
Ain't that peculiar
A peculiarity.

from *Ain't That Peculiar*

How can I possibly describe the anger and frustration I now feel daily when I confront the unwillingness of my body to walk, talk, swallow, chew, hear, smile, or move properly? The speech impediment that I have is maddening in its ability to turn any external evidence of my charm or intelligence into the type of drivel that a bunch of chimps would laugh at. My vocal cords are paralyzed; I have to yell in order to be heard over a distance of a few feet. My lips and tongue no longer want to move correctly. My speech is garbled, as well as inaudible. As a consequence, I can be thinking of a great joke or put-down, but all I can produce is an ineffective semblance of my conception. I am left feeling like a little human fission bomb: my most sophisticated thoughts and feelings are ready to implode within my already damaged brain.

The problem becomes one of deciding whether to keep on fighting. Ultimate death seems a certainty. Neurologic limitations make life unbearable. I continue to adjust to these limitations, but my list of neurologic problems grows longer each week. The tumor is on a blitzkrieg, each cancer cell like a miniature panzer tank plowing through the Poland of my brain. The tumor makes me look, feel, and act as if I was a concentration camp victim. Auschwitz's horrors sound similar to those induced by my brain tumor. The anguish of Auschwitz was compounded by each internee's knowledge that his or her pain was arbitrary—rooted in the capricious and wanton racism of his society. I share a similar perspective. I too am an arbitrary victim.

In my year of medical school, I was struck by the phenomenal beauty, complexity, and strength of the human immune system. I have since had to reconcile this knowledge with the incredible number of Americans (one out of four) who will develop cancer during their lifetime. There is only one logical reason that explains why this intricate defense mechanism is failing to protect us on a societal scale. We are being bombarded by carcinogens. Everything we eat, the water we drink, the clothes we wear, every damn breath we take, everything, is loaded with carcinogens and represents an assault on our immune systems. It is no wonder that one of four Americans will develop a detectable cancer. I would be willing to bet that the actual incidence of cancer is much higher than one out of four. If a careful enough autopsy was done, we would find a cancer in almost everyone, at least everyone who lives in this polluted, chemical-filled, toxic world of ours.

You see, I know how I got cancer. During the year prior to the appearance of my first symptom, I was exposed to benzene and xylene at the laboratory where I worked. Both of these chemicals have been implicated in carcinogenesis. I was also exposed to osmium tetroxide. This chemical has not been tested for carcinogenicity but is extremely toxic. Add to this exposure a lengthy and profound depression (no money, no women, would I get into med school?, how would I pay for med school?, did I even want to go to med school?), and at the same time a low resistance to disease (four to six hours of sleep per night, lots of coffee, an average American diet, plenty of stress). It's no wonder that my body broke under the strain and vomited up a brain tumor.

My rigid adherence to the program I learned at the health farm did me little good. The diet and enemas made me feel more energetic for a few weeks but my symptoms roared full speed ahead. Neurologically, I worsened noticeably. I made a frantic, last-ditch effort to receive immunotherapy. To date, this has not helped me, but I haven't given it a full chance. My heart just isn't in it anymore. Round fifteen is over and the other guy is too big and too strong for me. I want to taste real food again before I die, and I don't care if the tumor likes hamburgers as much as I do. I've done my hard time. I don't want to be a lifer cancer patient. I've met too many of them at the immunotherapy clinic, in my cancer support group, and down on the health farm. They are as sick as dogs, and they have spouses whose daily job is to attend to their many needs. They believe in Jesus and they are positive that they will get better. They are extremely well informed about the ten billion nontraditional approaches to the treatment of cancer. Laetrile, megavitamins, TumorX... the whole thing gets so absurd.

Cancer has eaten up enough of my time and energy. It has consumed enough of the resources of my friends and family. I hear about old pals from high school or medical school who are out in the world having babies, doing well in a career, or just taking a nice camping trip—and I can't stand it. I'm so jealous. A good day for me is one where I don't fall down while walking. I get excited when I have enough vocal clarity to get the information operator to understand me after less than three repetitions. Life is here to be lived! I'm losing myself steadily, piece by piece, as I sit in my bedroom, watching life unfold in front of me through the newspaper, TV, and the visitors who come to cheer me up.

It's all part of the narcissism inherent in the "Why-Me-Syndrome" that every cancer patient goes through. As though I'm so special and important that there has to be a reason for my illness. Well, as a dues-paying veteran of long standing (two years; it seems like so much more) in this here ole "war against cancer," it no longer intrigues me to try and answer that question. There is no good answer to "why me." Why not me? Cancer doesn't give a shit. It doesn't matter what religion, color, sex, or nationality I am. It doesn't care which medical school I was attending, how many friends I have, what a great guy I am, or any of that.

I have been asking "why me" every day for over two years. I don't care anymore why my body is in such a poor state. I just want the whole thing to end. I don't want to fall down in public anymore. I don't want to sit at parties without being able to speak, smiling like an imbecile at everybody's jokes to convince them that I'm not depressed. I don't want to enter into any more political arguments in which I can't express myself. I watch other people walking and talking with ease and I yearn to be like them again, to recover my voice, my left arm and leg, and my right eye. These were all given to me at birth, goddammit, and I mourn their passing like a spurned lover. Give me a new arm, leg, and voice and I'd be out there doing something. I'd be back in school or on a job, or working as a volunteer. I could be enjoying myself, traveling, going to movies, or eating in a fucking restaurant instead of sitting here watching these four walls as I feel my brain being munched away by this damn tumor.

I purposely had set myself up to give back more to my society than most of the average assholes walking around out there. It's a damn shame that this cancer is going to shut down my short life. It's an obscene waste, and I'm so angry about it I could scream. Well, almost. If I do scream now it comes out like a hoarse whisper and I end up with a sore throat and nothing else to show for the effort ....

When I'm up in that special part of heaven reserved for good Jewish socialists who died too young, I don't ever want to look down and see any of you guys arguing about whether life is worthwhile. My perspective, as I watch the curtain descend inexorably on my last act, is that I could spend years deeply immersed in millions of different things. I could read Polish history for months. I could listen to Bird's horn for a few years. I wonder how many decades it would take to really understand Marx. I'm going to miss it all so much: the clean smell of cool air after a good hard rain, the excitement of opening up a birthday present, the feeling of cracking a brand new book. I'm going to miss Miles Davis's trumpet, with its violently subdued sound that can chill you to death. I'm going to miss that little warm tingle in my spine when I hear a righteous old blues song. And Aretha Franklin, Al Green, James Brown, Lady Day, and Dizzy, Trane, Lester

Young...I shouldn't have let myself get started because this could get out of control! And don't forget Beethoven, oh shit, don't forget him. And Bach. And Mozart—well, I haven't listened to enough of him because I haven't had enough goddam time, godammit. I mean twenty-eight years just isn't enough, especially when you spend the first twenty-five with your head up your ass and the last three with cancer. Oh, and I'll miss bananas with cream, and Scrabble, and championship boxing matches, and driving in a car, and hamburgers cooked over a fire (with slabs of cheese, onions, and tomatoes), and the sound of crickets outside my window at night, and the feeling of cracking a good joke, and touching the woman in my life, and feeling the warmth of the sun as I lie on a quiet stretch of beach, and the feeling of nice new clothes, and Mexican vacations, and all of my friends, and my beautiful sister and brother, and my folks, and my lovely lady friend, honey, you're like a piece of Apple Pan apple pie—I never get enough of you. I'm going to miss reading the front page and the sports section, and I'm going to miss the sound of laughter, and the smell of food cooking, and the sound of music, and people, and traveling, and mountains, and friends, and, and, and...

It took cancer to show me that the truly important things in life are the trivialities that are usually taken for granted—all of the small repetitive rituals of life that we experience without even giving them a thought. Every year at my friend Joe's house, they take down the

Christmas tree in the late afternoon, during the break between the Rose Bowl and the Orange Bowl. I head over there at the appropriate time to participate in this annual event. The "moving of the tree ceremony" has now taken on almost religious overtones. I'm going to miss doing that, not because it's fun or that it gives me pleasure, or that it has any intrinsic value to me whatsoever. There's just something touching about this yearly marking of time. Something about it reminds me that life doesn't lead us in a straight line toward our goals. Life is like a merry-go-round. The ride takes you 'round and 'round and up and down. The trick is to learn how to appreciate the ride for its inherent qualities. I first understood this when I was twenty-four. After years of searching for a career, I realized that it didn't make a damn bit of difference what I finally chose to do. I would have enjoyed being a doctor, or a journalist, or a film director. The important questions in life are answered by how we do things, not the things we do.

Life isn't static, it's a process. I have more respect for a good plumber than a bad doctor. I have garnered a bit of peace in my short stay here on earth. I've learned that every day offers something to make life worthwhile. Generally, that something is so small that we overlook it. I'm not trying to be naïve: I know life can be incomprehensibly painful, unfair, and cruel. All I'm saying is that it's usually the small things that make life worth living.

I never gave a serious thought to my mortality until well into my illness. I saw a therapist for a year in an effort to piece together the jigsaw puzzle that I had become. He thought that dealing with mortality was the whole name of the game—the root of the anger, neuroses, maladaptive behaviors, and self-destructiveness of many people.

I opt for a more socioeconomic analysis, yet his point is well taken. Most of us spend time denying death's inevitability. The mere mention of the word provokes anxiety. Everybody runs scared. Doctors are digging in; there's a war on against my disease. Well, I've got good news from the front lines. As close as I've been to death, which lately has been awfully close, I've found nothing to be nervous about. I don't know what the hell death is. I hope it's like a nice rest, or making love, or an endless softball game. Maybe it's like good music: all you do is sit back, relax, and let the tunes move and groove you. It's probably nothingness, which is a hard thing for humans to conceptualize.

So why do I get scared? Why do I have nightmares and talk in my sleep? Over two years of cancer and I'm still scared to death. I mean I'm still scared of death. Pretty soon now I'm going to be so scared of life that its antithesis will become attractive. I wish it hadn't happened to me while I was so damn young. "Only the good die young," says the song. Well, I must be a fucking saint, my God, what a strange turn my life has taken! My imminent death has become my life. Don't think you're hiding anything from me. I know what you're thinking. I know you're out there watching...waiting. The sand in the hourglass is running out! Don't think I don't know that....

I've harbored fantasies of taking a fascist bullet in the cause of the socialist revolution. I can see myself dying a quick death from a tropical disease while working as a guerilla doctor in an undeveloped country. I can picture myself dying as an old man from a fatal heart attack, following a distinguished career in medicine. I just can't quite fathom the inevitability of perishing slowly from this cancer rotting out my brain. It feels so undignified.

Friends of mine often allude to the aura of drama that surrounds a person with a brain tumor. We've all read too many cheap novels and seen too many crappy movies where a brain tumor is utilized as the ultimate dramatic vehicle. The documentary version is slightly different. My tumor is an X-rated obscenity, a waste of my time and spirit. There is nothing dramatic about the suffering slowness with which this motherfucker is putting me down for the count.

My neurological functions have been messed up for so long that I am constantly surprised by how easy it is for normal people to walk, talk, swallow, chew, and all of the other thousands of things that I can no longer do properly. My frustration is reflected in my dreams, in which I do simple things endlessly. Sometimes in these dreams I walk through beautiful meadows for hours. Sometimes I run along the sand of a Mexican beach. One night I had a dream that I was in the grocery store with my mom. All of a sudden I could walk! I walked up and down those aisles for weeks. Canned vegetables, ice cream, peanut butter, bananas, wine, yogurt, chicken wings—fill that basket to the brim, Ma! I can walk again! I'm cured!

Some fundamental part of me cannot believe or accept that I will never be able to take a hard run in the outfield with everybody watching me and nobody thinking I have a chance in hell of getting to the ball; but I'm running hard with my hand and arm stretched out across my body as far as they will go, and then I make a dive and say a quick prayer and there is the sound of the ball hitting the leather of my mitt, THWACK! I've made the catch! My body hits the ground hard after my leap but I don't feel a thing because of the adrenaline pumping through my veins. All the girls are going to fall in love with me. All the guys are going to talk about my great catch for the rest of their lives. They'll tell their children and their grandchildren—my catch will live on forever. It's pure, unadulterated mother-and-father-love, a giant wave of tingly good feeling.

After the inning is over I go back to the bench where all of my friends are congratulating me with "Wow....great catch..." and "good grab, Jimmy." I say, "Yeah, thanks," real low-key as if I don't even remember what they're referring to. This is only one of the "trivial" life experiences that this brain tumor has robbed me of—with all the drama of a Super 8 porno flick.

□

After living with cancer for two years, I reached the point where I was considered "terminally ill." I don't know how I crossed this line, or exactly when it happened. My brain tumor had regrown, radiation therapy hadn't worked, the doctors became distinctly cooler in their dealings with me. I decided that before I totally gave up on modern medicine I would go to UCLA's Biomedical Library. I would read everything I could get my hands on about my tumor. I had never wanted to read this information before. I considered many of my doctors to be intellectually and psychologically limited by their slavish attachment to statistics. I was convinced that my doctors were wearing blinders created by reading too many books, charts, graphs, and statistics. What did any of this ancient history have to do with me? I was Jim Slotnick (S...L...O...T...N...I...C...K, yeah, just like it sounds), and I was going to beat this thing no matter what the experts said. I wasn't going to let any foreboding statistics get me down.

My visit to the biomedical library convinced me that I had been incorrect in my critique of the doctors. It became apparent as I read the medical literature that I was wrong about my doctors being slaves to their statistics. In fact, my doctors apparently hadn't paid attention to the statistics at all. The plain fact was that none of the conventional treatment modalities do much good for brain tumors. There are some very specific kinds of brain tumors which respond well to surgery or radiation therapy. I would recommend that anyone who has one of these types of tumors stick with the doctors. However, for the vast majority of brain tumors, modern medical techniques are not going to help much. More likely, doctors are only going to exacerbate the problem with their painful, dangerous, and destructive treatments. Some of the diagnostic procedures alone can make life miserable for the patient. Doctors end up harming some patients who otherwise might have improved had they been allowed to pursue nonconventional therapies. By the time most people turn to megavitamin, immuno-, or nutritional therapies, their bodies and spirits have been eroded by "modern" medical techniques.

The confusion of medical doctors dedicated to "modern" therapeutic techniques is reflected in a curious contradiction. When it comes to justifying their techniques, these doctors are happy to utilize anecdotal evidence. Simultaneously, they criticize alternative therapies for resting upon an anecdotal foundation. A large part of medical education is based on scientific rationalism and therefore dismisses anecdotal evidence. It is not valid to use patient histories as proof that a particular treatment works. Contentions about treatment efficacy must be based on experimental evidence, utilizing the proper controls. I have encountered numerous physicians who are more than willing to criticize Linus Pauling's book, *Vitamin C and the Common Cold* for its dependence on anecdotal evidence. Where are the experiments, the tables, the charts and graphs? We don't care if it works— we want to see some hard facts, some data, some test results. These very same doctors were brazenly making treatment recommendations to me based on the most crass anecdotes imaginable. "Well, I once had a patient who responded real well to...," or "Yeah, I heard about a Dr. Putzbag in San Francisco who does really good things for brain tumors...."

I get furious when I realize that my body, with its "interesting" tumor, has essentially been used as fuel for the thirsty engines of the capital-intensive health care industry. Once I developed this tumor I became an object to be poked, X-rayed, CAT-scanned, irradiated, photographed, and otherwise unmercifully tortured. Cancer is good business—tumors are a "growth industry." Cancer patients need care, the more expensive the better. Every unfortunate who gets cancer justifies the need for more CAT scanners, radiation machines, research grants, hospitals, and medical schools. Tumors are costly to detect, evaluate, and treat. All of these processes generate capital. My tumor kills me but keeps the economy alive.

It is testimony to the perverse internal logic of capitalism that the very same companies, which are polluting the environment with carcinogens, derive profit from health care provided for cancer victims. I have an idea that would begin to change this situation: simply make cancer unprofitable. Make the corporations pay their fair share of the medical expenses of cancer patients whose tumors are attributable to their products. A concerted attack must also be made on the collusive relationship between government and industry, which causes our environment to become filled with carcinogens. This will entail no less than a fundamental alteration of our social structure.

□

Samuel Epstein brilliantly illustrates in *The Politics of Cancer* that cancer may never turn out to be a curable disease, but we already know that it is highly preventable. Is this a paranoid vision? I was a medical student when my cancer began. I had bitten into the logic of scientific rationalism hook, line, and sinker. I wanted to believe that my doctors had the answers. I was scared, God knows that I was scared shitless. I didn't want to die—I was too young to go. I was afraid, but I was not paranoid. I was only trying to reconcile what I had learned in medical school about the complexity of my immune system with the fact that I now had this disease.

I am not trying to divest myself of individual responsibility for my brain tumor. I drank too much coffee, placed myself under too much stress, and I didn't have the proper emotional outlets. I acknowledge that on some level this brain tumor is my problem as an individual. It's not my mom's problem, Ronald Reagan's problem, or even God's problem. It's mine, all mine. But the fact remains that at least one out of four and perhaps one out of three Americans will develop cancer during their lifetime. Statistics like these make cancer society's problem—everyone's problem, whether we like it or not.

CHAPTER THIRTEEN

Riches and Fame

At my tender age of twenty-eight, the imminence of death brings on feelings of anger, sadness, and frustration. My emotions reflect the pain of life's unfairness. I have also experienced a freedom and exhilaration that comes from having one foot squarely planted in the next world. Perhaps this freedom explains my choice of activity during my last days: horse-race handicapping. My brother Jon has always been a racing fanatic, and his interest in "the sport of kings" rubbed off on me. The track is a fascinating world filled with horses, the smell of easy money, and the constant refrain of "should have done this, but…" I should have had good health, but I didn't. The doctors should have had a cure for my cancer, but they didn't. I felt like I fit in nicely with all the other losers out at the track.

My first horseplay was made strictly on intuition. My roommate's name is Andrew, so I plunked two bucks across the board on a nag named Andrew 'n Me. I didn't even bother to go to the track. I gave money to my brother to place the bet. This maiden colt came home a winner at 6 to 1 and I was up twenty-seven dollars!

Hey, this was easy! I pick a name out of the paper and I'm twenty-seven dollars richer! Big number 4, Andrew 'n Me, with Valenzuela on top. What a killing! At this rate I'll be a rich man before I die.

I decided that I would actually go to the track the next day, instead of giving my brother the money to bet. This was a red-letter day in my neurologic decline. I conceded that I could no longer walk safely—I had already taken a number of hard spills—so my brother rented a wheelchair for the Hollywood Park excursion. The first thing I noticed about the crowd at the track was the large number of people who were confined to wheelchairs. I was by far the youngest, but I felt comfortable there among my people! There were probably no more wheelchair people there than at any other public gathering of comparable size. It was just that I was noticing them for the first time. Well, we wheelchair people were big losers out in the real world, but we could win at the track as easily as anyone else who could say "two dollars across the board on number 10." Which is exactly what I said before the second race of my first wheelchair day at the track. I bet on Daring Anne. She was a three-year-old maiden filly, going off at 12 to 1. After fighting off a stretch challenge from Tribal Rites, Daring Anne cruised home a wire-to-wire winner in her very first race!

I was forty dollars richer and ecstatic. There is no feeling in the world like picking a longshot winner at the track. I felt as if I had tapped into the flow of objective reality. Perhaps I had helped to create that reality. Maybe God Himself was involved. He took a quick glance down from heaven, saw my six bucks on number 10, and charged that filly up with enough speed to win the race. I watched her victory on a TV screen out at the track. The race drilled itself into my mind as I watched the replays.

The aspect of the experience that I enjoyed most was the process of picking Daring Anne to win the race. When someone at the track knows what he's doing, this is called handicapping. Physically, I'm about as handicapped as a person can be, but this doesn't give me any edge in choosing horses. My technique is eclectic. I combine a rational, objective perusal of the racing form with instincts about the horses' names, jockeys, numerology, what I ate for breakfast, random chance, and last-minute intuition. All of these factors are combined with a complete disdain for whether I win or lose on any one bet. I like to leave at the end of the day with the track's money, but I'm careful to only make bets that I'm comfortable with. I don't want to be upset when I lose. On Daring Anne day, I lost every subsequent wager I made but left the track a winner. I had paid for admission, a program, hot dogs, and a racing form. I had bet on every race, and I was still up ten bucks. Nothing sensational but a good day at the track, nonetheless.

My fantasies of invincibility were rudely shattered on my next venture out to Hollywood Park. That's one of the best things about horse racing—it's a constant test of the appropriateness of one's self-image. It's hard to maintain any illusions about beating the track or being smarter than the rest of the crowd, unless one is a consistent winner. There are nine races in a day's racing program. Nine chances a day to prove whatever you need to prove. Nine chances to be a winner or a loser. I have yet to meet the person who wins consistently at the track. I must assume that anyone who is intelligent enough to master handicapping has long since gone on to bigger and better things.

In the third race exacta, one gloomy Saturday, I knew I had the top two horses. The winner, of course, would be Gringo Jim. He was my namesake and he had won his last race in a field of the same caliber horses. Earlier in the season, he had been involved in a $1,500 exacta with a horse named Nat's Penny. My mom's name is Penny. Joshie Boy was my choice for the place bet. I knew a great little two-year-old kid named Josh, whose parents called him Joshie. Joshie Boy had beaten a similar field as a 16 to 1 longshot his last time out. I liked everything about this bet. Both of my horses were aptly named; Pincay and Hawley, two excellent jockeys, were on board, and my horses were breaking from the second and third post positions—good for saving ground. There was no way I could lose—this exacta was all mine! It was too easy!

Well, things in life never work out the way they should. Joshie Boy ran a creditable race to finish a predictable second. Inexplicably, Gringo Jim petered out at the head of the stretch. The number 6 horse, a 20 to 1 longshot with the unpronounceable name of Tao's Tewa Dancer, grabbed the lead and held on gamely for the win.

My next visit to the track was more successful. Oooooweeeee, I had a feeling this was going to be a good day, and it was! As I was driving to Hollywood Park with my mom, I handicapped the first two races. They looked easy: Sandcrab or Family Fox had to win the first, and Capichi threatened to lap the forgettable field in the second race. He was entered in a $25,000 claimer—taking a nosedive in class. Ten minutes later, I watched my fantasies unfold. Sandcrab withstood a strong challenge in the stretch from Long Gyland, a longshot with no business even being in the race. The photo finish was as close as I've ever seen, but Sandcrab emerged the winner by less than a nose. In the second race, Capichi made the other horses look like they were standing still, and fired off to an easy 5½ length victory. I had done it! I had won the daily double and $17.60. The money was a paltry sum and had no bearing on my exhilaration. I felt omniscient! I had just predicted the outcome of not one but two races—two winners in a row. I was invincible, all-knowing, all-seeing, a prognosticator of the highest rank. I was so smart, I thought to myself....

Oh, I was smart all right, but not smart enough to stay away from the track. I would return on numerous occasions, and come back more humble and poorer each time. Then, disaster struck. I decided to protect against my losses at the track with some selective wagers on pro football games. I had a friend who knew a bookie, and all I had to do was pick up the phone and my bet was down! I was going to be patient and wait for the right game. After a few weeks, it came. The Pittsburgh Steelers were playing the Seattle Seahawks. I took Pittsburgh, gave away 6 points to Seattle, and congratulated myself on an easy seventy-five dollar victory. Football was so much simpler than a horse race. First of all, there were only two teams, in comparison with the eight to twelve thoroughbreds in the average horse race. These two teams had usually played each other previously, a number of times. These prior meetings provided a clear picture of how the teams matched up in head-to-head competition. Pittsburgh had beaten Seattle on eight straight previous occasions, and there was no reason to suspect that this game would be any different. Pittsburgh entered the contest with an unblemished record of 3 wins, 0 losses. They had a solid team of veterans who were threatening to recapture their Super Bowl form of the 1970s. Seattle was a mediocre team mired in quarterback controversies and coaching problems. Going into the game against Pittsburgh, they had an undistinguished record of 1-2. There was absolutely no way that Pittsburgh could lose. The point spread made it a little tricky, but I figured the Steelers were good for a twenty-point victory. I felt safe giving away the 6 points.

Early reports out of Seattle were not encouraging: the Seahawks were up 3-0 in the second quarter. Okay, no big deal. Seattle was probably playing the game of its life for the home crowd. I knew that the Steelers were good for at least three touchdowns, so I wasn't too concerned. Then the bombshell hit. Terry Bradshaw, the Pittsburgh quarterback, had suffered a shoulder separation in the first quarter and would be out for the game. Terry Bradshaw out for the game? This was a disaster on the order of the *Hindenburg*, the *Titanic*, and the San Francisco earthquake! The Steeler offense without Bradshaw was like a ship without a captain. I had the nauseous feeling of a man who had just flushed seventy-five dollars down the toilet by accident. The Seahawks ended up victors, shutting out the Steelers 16-0. I vowed never to bet on a football game again.

The next day, I broke my vow. Monday Night Football featured a matchup between the underdog Tampa Bay Bucs and the Super Bowl-bound Miami Dolphins. I didn't like the idea of giving my seventy-five dollars to a bookie, so I fell into the classic trap of the inexperienced gambler: I threw good money after bad. I bet on Miami and gave away 5½ points to Tampa. To make a long story short, Tampa Bay soundly thrashed the Dolphins. Now I owed the sleazeball bookie $150. I had spent all of my track money for the next three weeks. I was an impetuous fool, and I berated myself for several hours until I remembered my tumor. My tumor was the problem, not the gambling. The gambling was an escape. It was supposed to help me forget, but losing was starting to get on my nerves.

□

I should have accepted the clear signal of my football betting errors and stayed far away from further wagering, but I couldn't resist the temptation. Pretty soon I was back at the track. They say a fool and his money are soon parted. Well, I must have been ready to be cast in a Shakespearean comedy. My money started disappearing with frightful regularity as I made one stupid bet after another. The low point was reached during the eighth race at Hollywood Park, on Saturday, December 4, 1982, 4:30 P.M. This race was the sixth running of the "Meteor Handicap" and featured a field of the fastest sprinters in the country. It was as predictable as any race was ever going to be. Chinook Pass had recently set the world record over a distance of five furlongs and was going to win. Dave's Friend had just placed third in the "California Sprint Championship," had speed to burn, and everybody in the place knew he would finish second. So what was the logical bet? A five-dollar exacta wager from Chinook's Pass to Dave's Friend would bring in $27.50. It was a bet crying out to be made. It couldn't have been more obvious.

I was at the track with my friend Dave, so of course I put twenty dollars to win on Dave's Friend. I knew that my horse wasn't going to win, but I made the bet anyway. I knew that Chinook Pass was a better horse. Chinook Pass burned by my horse at the first quarter pole and never faltered. Dave's Friend finished second, like I knew he would. Chinook Pass won the race easily. I was out twenty dollars.

I sat in front of the track's TV monitor, which was suspended from the ceiling. I was in my wheelchair. I watched replay after replay of the race. The result never changed. Over and over again, Chinook Pass won and Dave's Friend finished second. Any stumblebum who could read the racing form would have predicted this result. After this race I decided that it was all over between me and the track. I could get more entertainment value for my money by going to the movies. The races were a nice obsession for a while, but losing consistently made me think too much about all of the things I was trying to forget. Losing bets at the races reminded me of cancer.

I began to see myself being nipped by my tumor at the wire, and I didn't need that. Winning, losing, dying in the stretch, doctors, jockeys, nurses, trainers—they all became one big mess in my mind. I couldn't sort anything out. I started to get scared. The whole thing was too close, just a TV screen away. It was inevitable. Chinook Pass would win that damn race every time. Dave's Friend would always finish second. Inevitably. I would always bet on Dave's Friend, because I was out at the track with my buddy Dave. That's as good a reason as any, isn't it? And inevitably, I would lose my money. It was all too predictable, like my death. I looked up at the TV screen. Chinook Pass was winning the race again.

CHAPTER FOURTEEN

All's Well That Ends Well

In a week I'm due to celebrate birthday
number twenty-eight but I can't get all that excited about
it. I usually love my birthdays, but I'm too cancerous right
now to get up for this one. I'm too filled with cancer to
have room left for a celebration of my birth. This year, the
day has become relegated to the status of a mathematical
marker, a signpost that tells me I've done too much hard
time for any young person to bear. December 18, 1982, I
will have lived 10,220 days. My heart will have completed
6,160,220,000 beats, give or take a few hundred thousand.
I've put over 60,000 miles on my VW bug. I've hitchhiked
a few thousand miles. My body has converted more than
a few tons of food into the best fertilizer money can buy.
I have made one documentary film, and now I've written my memoir. Throw in a million smiles, a few small
lies, two thousand cups of coffee. Add a million dreams,
a trillion thoughts, ideas, and hopes. Put in some tears,
some fears, and one big wish. I wish to God I didn't have
this tumor chewing on my brain. I wish that I didn't have
cancer.

□

Who keeps lengthening my damn hallway? When the urge to urinate becomes overwhelming, I have to get up and go pee. Now that may not be any big deal for you "normals" out there. For those of us less fortunate souls, whose left legs have the stability of last week's meat loaf, the trip down the hall becomes a journey fraught with Dantean potentialities.

I am totally convinced that carpenters come into my apartment and lengthen my hall when I'm not here. What other explanation can there be? I mean, the damn bathroom is beginning to look like it's a football field away! I feel as if it takes me light years to make the trip. Will the Dodgers still be playing in Los Angeles when I come back from my pee?

Let's say I'm sitting here in my room, on my couch, happy as a clam ... and I get the urge to pee. What does a normal person do in this situation? He gets up, goes to the bathroom, and pees. What did I do for the first twenty-six years of my life? I went to the bathroom, peed, and I forgot about it. Now I've got a brain tumor: my left leg refuses to work. What do I do now? I sit. I sit and I wait and I hope that the urge will go away, or that I'll die first, or that I'll just forget about it. The urge to pee, however, is like an irrepressible debt collector. . . . Hello, here I am again! At some point it becomes too burdensome to ignore. So here I am with this enormous urge, oh God, I've really GOT to go soon, I'm gonna turn blue and pee in my pants if I'm not careful, this is really bad, I've gotta

go bad, real bad, real, REAL bad now—and the commitment to the trek down the hall is finally made.

I'm usually sitting in my room when this process
begins. Step one in my journey is to move from a sitting
position on the couch to an erect stance next to the couch.
After failing this maneuver a number of times and end-
ing up in an undignified heap on the floor, I have now
perfected a method of making this transition properly.
Suspended on the wall above my couch are four book-
shelves. I grab the lowest one with my right hand. At the
same time, I twist my lower body so that I'm perched
on the edge of the couch. I'm ready to make my move.
Ughghghhhhh! I pull down hard with my right arm and
I push down hard with my right leg and somehow, a few
seconds later, I'm up! I'm standing securely with my right
hand locked in a tight grip on that shelf. I'm concentrating hard on that right hand, that's my stability hand.
Without that hand I'd only be standing on my two legs,
except in my case it's one good leg and one bum leg, so
I'm substituting my good hand for my bum leg.

That frigging bathroom looks miles away down that
hall. I swear to God, somebody is messing around with
my apartment when I'm not here. When I catch them in
the act, I'm gonna beat the living hell out of them! But
for now, I must take care of first things first.

The next hurdle I face is getting to the hall entrance.
This is a moderately easy operation. I lean against the
bookshelf that I'm already holding with my right hand

and perform the required five steps to the hall. My right hand slides along the shelf for stability. My left leg doesn't take whole steps. I drag it with me. At the entrance to the hall I switch my right hand from the shelf to the wall. I am now securely planted in the hallway entrance. My right hand is on the wall to my right. My good leg is supporting my body. My bad leg is dangling next to my penis, which is busy blocking off the raging tide of urine that threatens to spill down my pants. I notice that the carpenters have been working on the hall again. I don't remember it being anywhere near this long the last time I took a pee.

Down the hall I go. I am leaning on the wall to my right for support. There is a light switch in the hall. It is located on the left-hand wall, about four paces from the entrance to the bathroom. I can switch it on if I need to. To accomplish this, I have to use my right hand. To free this hand I have to lean my body against the left-hand wall. This is easily done. The whole procedure of turning on the light only takes me ten seconds. Bing! Let there be light! Step with the right leg, drag the left leg, step again with the right, drag the left. Step. Drag. Step, drag. Step, drag, step, drag, plunk, shhhhh, plunk, shhhhh, plunk, shhhhh. The entire hall is not much more than ten yards in length. It takes me five minutes to make the journey.

The last three yards are the most difficult. My room-mate and I have parked our bikes there. I haven't had the coordination or energy to ride my bike in months.

The hallway to the bathroom is the only logical storage place for the bicycles. How many times did I pass them without a thought when I was healthy? How often does my roommate unthinkingly walk to the bathroom now, unaware of the potential hazards of those seemingly innocent bikes? He probably thinks that they're good machines, benevolent transports, nonpolluting, energy-efficient vehicles. Well, they're not! They're traps, spider webs of metal designed to hurt and maim disabled people, and they're probably put there by the same sons of bitches who keep lengthening my damn hallways! I slide by them carefully. They lean against the wall, on the right. I avoid them by sliding on the left-hand wall.

Now comes the hardest part. I'm at the door of the bathroom. I remove my right hand from the wall and place it on the doorknob. This move has many inherent dangers. I could miss the doorknob with my hand and fall to the floor. The door itself might swing on its hinges, and I could once again end up on the floor. The shoe on my useless left foot might catch on the molding on the floor, and I could trip and fall. I'm thinking about all three of these horrible options as I move my hand from the wall to the door. All three scenarios would leave me crumpled on the floor in a little Jewish mound. This must be avoided at all costs.

Entrance into the bathroom has been achieved! The three feet to the toilet can be covered in less than ten steps. Now I can finally let my welled-up urine flow freely. My penis has held back the sea of pee as long as it can. My bladder is swelling, my teeth are clenched, and I'm dripping with sweat from the combined effort of the journey down the hall and holding back my ocean of piss. I know that I've got to take the last step in my journey as quickly as I can, before the pee starts to overflow down my leg. And what is the last step? Well, a normal guy would just whip out his penis and stand over the bowl and pee to his heart's delight. But not Pontine Glioma Man, not tumor-head, not me! I no longer have the ability to stand at the toilet for that long. I might fall on the floor and break my ass into a million pieces. What can I do? Well...I pee sitting down. Okay, so now you know my secret! James Slotnick, James Ely Slotnick, man about town, bon vivant, former medical student, pees just like a g——, gi——, pees just like a girl!

And do you want to know whose fault this is? It's those damn carpenters who've been working on my hall when I'm not here! If I ever catch them I'm going to break their necks.

□

I wish that I could sum it all up with a single word. I've heard it said that every action holds within it the key to the individual. The truly sensitive person can see someone else's essence in the blink of an eyelid or the motion of a single step. Most of us can tell a great deal about a person from their handshake. What can I say that will tie this all together in a nice bundle? What single word would make it all come clear? What would my word be?

Cancer. No, that's not really me. I know that my cancer is made up of cells that are genetically me, but I think of this tumor as only expressing one part of me, and not a particularly pleasant part at that. The cancer is an invader, a foreigner—it isn't me. No, cancer is a big word in my life, but not the biggest.

Baseball. That's a nice word, but it's not an important word. It's just a game. A silly game played by nine men on a team, playing on a diamond-shaped field. I like baseball very much, but it's too trivial to sum up my memoirs. I have begun to see my life as a trivial affair, so perhaps baseball would be a good word. It's pleasant—I can't object to it. I love to play and watch the game, but "baseball" doesn't have the scope to sum up anything.

Disabled. What an ugly, God-forsaken word. Disability, inability, lack of ability, it all adds up to the sad fact that I can't do anything physical anymore. I can't use my left arm because it's paralyzed. My left leg is paralyzed and I can't walk. My vocal cords are paralyzed and I can't speak. The right side of my face is paralyzed so I've only got half of my smile. My right ear no longer hears, and my right eyelid won't close, and my mouth won't open easily. My right eye won't—oh shit, it's easier to describe the parts that do work. My left ear, my nose, and my penis are still serving me with distinction and valor—sometimes even heroically.

One can maintain a semblance of humanity with just one good ear, a nose, and a penis, if given wonderful family members and friends who will help. They can do things to make life easier: lift you into the tub in the morning and lift you out when you're done, put you on the couch after your bath, put on your socks and shoes, put on your shirt, and feed you. *Uggggggghhhh*. *Disabled* is a mean word which actually means dependence and lack of control. It also means that I now pee into a bottle because the walk to the bathroom has become so difficult. It's a horrible word that I know as well as anyone.

The most bizarre aspect of the word disabled is the suddenness and completeness with which it entered my life. I'm a jogger, I was a jogger, I will always be a jogger. I would love to jog five miles right now! I can't even lift myself up off this couch, but in my mind's eye I'm still a runner, I still love to run!

My left arm is paralyzed. I have to put a jacket on this arm first, with my right hand. But twenty-six years of normalcy cannot be denied. I always put my jackets on right arm first, and then I remember. Ding! I am now disabled. My left arm is paralyzed. I've got to use my good right arm to thread my bad left arm through the arm hole. My left arm has to go in first.

Disabled. Nope, not a good summation word. Once again, it only describes a portion of the story.

There is a fundamental part of me that is not at all disabled. Recently, I stayed up writing from 11:30 A.M. to 4:30 P.M. Laurie is my witness. I didn't move from the couch, pee, eat, nap, or speak during this time. I wrote for five straight hours. I didn't look at the clock. I didn't move the pen from the paper. I can't make the five-yard trek from my couch to the bed without assistance, yet I have the ability to write like a maniac, a crazy man, an amphetamine head. Two cups of coffee a day are enough fuel for this brain-damaged youth, risen out of the ghetto of Beverly Hills.... Well, "disabled" has been an absurdly important word in my recent days, but I would never, never use it to describe me. I'm on the disabled list. I'm out for the season. I'm temporarily on the shelf. But I'm not totally disabled. I can still think and I can still feel, and the only thing that will stop that will be death.

Death. An ugly word. It doesn't sum, it ends. It's an unavoidable word. Its imminence has spawned this memoir. I do not believe that anybody knows anything about it unless they are already dead, in which case their knowledge is useless to us warm ones living above ground (allow me to tenuously include myself). I've been studying death closely now for over two years. I'm a smart guy, and I haven't figured out the first thing about it. Intuition tells me that it's not a difficult thing to do, judging by all of the people who have successfully completed the task.

Am I scared? You can bet your house and car I am. I'm badly scared, scared out of my wits. I'm scared shitless, scared to death! However, death is not my summation word. Death is not the end of the line, it's just the end of the line for me. Hey, lots of people are going to have great memories of me. I've got a great pair of siblings to carry on the flame. Joe is going to ignite the revolution with his plays, Laurie will think of me lovingly for all of her days. I'm even going to have a baby or two named after me! Mom and Dad will always carry me in their hearts, and December 18 will always be my birthday. Lots of my friends will keep me in their thoughts, and people will read this and wonder about who I was. And life will go on. That's the strangest revelation of cancer/death. Life will go on. Without me? You bet. Life goes on, babies are born, people die in car accidents, the Dodgers win the Series, unemployment goes up, people study cancer, others get cancer, Mexican beach towns keep on having gorgeous sunsets, people get married, people get divorced, ships will sail, planes will fly, horses will run around racetracks while people place bets on them, businesses will open and close, and there's going to be a Cotton, Sugar, Rose, and Orange Bowl this year even if I die. "Death" is definitely not the best summation word—there is too much life around. My death is a relatively unimportant matter—not to be glorified out of proportion to its actual value.

There is no single word that conveys all that I want to share. That's why I am stringing together all of these words into my memoir. Maybe the cumulative effect of a lot of words hooked together will communicate some of my thoughts and feelings.

A number of years after high school, I hopped the freights with a couple of good friends. Berkeley to Sacramento, CA. A Sacramento overnight stay. Sacto to Davis, and Davis toward Portland, Oregon, by mistake. We caught our first ride from a train that was parked and we had our choice of cars. We opted for a wonderful old flatcar. During the ride we got drunk on cheap wine. I put my head down on the wooden floor of the car and watched as the countryside whisked by. The scenery was far better than anything I had ever seen from a car. There were no billboards, freeways, restaurants, or motels. Just wide-open vistas filled with nice green things to look at. Soon I was attending to the sound of the train on the track. It was my summation word: **clickety-clack, clickety-clack, clickety-clack, clickety-clack, clickety, clack, click, click, click, clack, click, clack, clickety-clack, click, clack, click, click, clack, click, clack, clickety-clack, clickety-clack, click clack, click clack, clack, click, clack, click, clack, clickety-clack, clickety-clack, clickety-clack, click, click, click, clack, click clack, clickety-clack, click, click click, clack, clack, clack...**

What a pulse beat, what a rhythm. I finally understood Elvis Jones's drumming—there's no repetition! The tempo, the speed, the motion of both the train and the music are constants, but within that framework there is plenty of room for improvisation. The train sounded just like Elvis—powerful, smooth, rhythmic, and cool. I'll go with the train sound to sum up everything. Clickety-clack, clickety, clickety, clack, click, click, clack, clack, clack...

Epilogue

So, dear reader, you feel cheated, don't you? Now you want to know whether I die, right? You've waded through the childhood memories, the political rhetoric, the adolescent fantasies. Everybody has a story about their doctors. You must be wondering what the message is in all of this. What's the point? Did I make it or not? I've decided to provide a number of different endings. You can choose the one you like.

"Jim Slotnick conquered his cancer and obtained a position as an assistant manager of a Radio Shack in Oroville, California. He is presently pursuing a degree in radio broadcast engineering through the mail."

"Jim Slotnick has successfully conquered cancer by accepting Jesus Christ into his heart. He presently owns a fast-food franchise in Wikieup, Arizona."

"Jim Slotnick's doctors have decided that none of his tests were conclusive about anything. In this light, they would like to subject him to a battery of new tests."

Die? What, me die? I can't die. I'm only twenty-eight and I've got bills to pay. I'm in debt up to my ass! I can't afford to die! Actually, if I do have to die, I'm going to be good at it. I've had a lot of practice. I started dying when

Epilogue

I was told I had cancer. Since then, I've died many times. I died every time I talked with somebody who had just been accepted into medical school. I died a little bit every time one of my friends from med school told me about the wards, the doctors, and the patients. I should be there on those wards. A little part of me dies every time I see somebody out jogging—hey, I used to do that. And I die when I remember that I can no longer play baseball and I will never be able to play baseball again. I die every time I look deep into my woman friend's beautiful blue eyes and see the kindness there. I think of how much fun we would have had, and I think of the jokes I could have cracked, and the birthdays, the camping trips, and the warm feeling of her sweet embrace. Sometimes when I'm staring deep into the blue of her iris I feel like I'm looking over the edge of a deep well. Inside the well is all of the love, warmth, and disappointment in the world. Her eyes reflect my pain, her anger mirrors my frustration.

"I shouldn't have this cancer," I say.

She agrees. It's obscene, unbelievable, it doesn't make any sense.

And then a little chunk inside of me fills up with tears and dies from the sadness.

□

I thought it would be important for you to know a little about the creatures who inhabit this memoir's dedication page. Obviously I'm nuts about them, otherwise their names wouldn't be there. Since I run the risk of boring you to death, I mean boring you to tears with sentimentality in this section, I will force myself to remain brief.

"Mom and Dad" refer to my biological parents. Notice that I have cleverly managed to avoid mentioning them up to this point. This in no way reflects their importance in my life. They are the original source of the strength that allows me to plug mulishly ahead, blind to the slings and arrows of outrageous misfortune. I wish I had thought of that myself.

"Sara" is my biological sister. We look very much alike. She is very beautiful and she is a fantastic artist. She is sensitive, loving, tender, womanly... alright, alright. I warned you about the sentimentality. She is a great cook, an excellent typist, a hard worker, a good Scrabble player. She has a new, extremely short, haircut. She looks great. I love her dearly.

"Jon" is my biological brother. He is verbal, funny, and very intelligent. He consistently kicks my ass in chess. He enjoys that very much. He's a pretty good cook. He will be phenomenally good at whatever he chooses to do with his life. Right now he doesn't know what that will be, although he is starting to lean towards journalism. He loves to gamble. He'll put money down on anything. Don't give him any spare cash! He is very handsome—even though he doesn't resemble me. He has a new, extremely short, haircut. It makes him look like a mass murderer. I hope it will grow out soon.

Epilogue

"Joe" is my biological best friend. He figures prominently in the preceding pages. (If you don't remember Joe, please reread the relevant sections. There will be a short quiz at the end of the hour.) Joe has an awesome intelligence. He is a playwright. The scope of his plays amazes me. He is the most loyal person I've ever met. He has the strongest life force that I have ever encountered. He gets his hair cut at barber shops even the greenest of marines would avoid.

"Laurie" is my biological sweetheart. We went out together for almost six months before she would admit that she liked me. I had kind of known it all along, so I wasn't too insecure about it. She is a wonderful person. She has stuck right by my side as I've been wasting away with cancer. She is warm, funny, strong, bright, and giving. She is the most nonjudgmental person I've ever met, yet she has a strong moral streak. She is very ignorant politically. She has terrible taste in movies. She has been so loyal and good to me that I am forever in her debt. Her hair looks great when it's not styled. She insists on blow-drying it every morning. I wish she wouldn't do that, but I'm crazy about her anyway. She is very beautiful.

□

Scarecrow: That's the trouble! I can't make up my mind.
I haven't got a brain...only straw. Oh, I'm a
failure because I haven't
got a brain.

Dorothy: What would you do with a brain if
you had one?

Scarecrow: Do? Why, if I had a brain I could...
I could while away the hours
Conferring with the flowers—
Consulting with the rain.
My head I'd be scratchin'
While my thoughts were busy hatchin'
If I only had a brain.
I'd be solving any riddle
For any indi-viddle
In trouble or in pain.

Dorothy: With the thought you'd be thinkin'
You could be another Lincoln
If you only had a brain.

Scarecrow: Oh I—
Could tell you why—
The ocean
Is near the shore.
I could think of things
I never thunk before;
And then I'd sit,
And think some more.

I would not be just a nothin'
My head all full of stuffin'
My heart all full of pain.
I would dance and be merry,
Life would be a thingaderry,
If only I had a brain.

—*The Wizard of Oz*

Postscript

JIM FINISHED WORKING ON THIS MANUSCRIPT the night of January 31, 1983. Remarkably, he died twenty-four hours later, a little after midnight, on February 2, 1983. Just as remarkable was the fact that, with the exception of his brief hospital visits for tests, Jim was dressed in street clothes and sitting up every day of his illness—ready to jog at the slightest sign of improvement.

For those of you who did not know Jim, this book will have to speak for him. Hopefully it will make you feel happy, sad, angry, curious, depressed, politicized, loving, sensitive, and a million other things. For those of us who were lucky enough to have known Jim, we have this book, and a host of great memories that will always be with us.

At the heart of the matter, Jim was one fine human being, and there is no way to rationalize, justify, or even understand his death. No written tribute could adequately express how courageous, proud, and dignified Jim was in his fight against his tumor. I think we can pay tribute to him, however, through our actions. Whenever we sacrifice a little time and energy to help somebody else, whenever we're honest, whenever we find humor in difficult situations, and whenever we refuse to stop fighting when the odds are overwhelmingly against us, we will be carrying on Jim's spirit.

JON SLOTNICK

The Jim Slotnick Fellowship in Medicine at Saban Community Clinic

Jim adored the Los Angeles Free Clinic. As a young medical student, his heart and eyes were opened by the spirit of the Clinic and by its motto: health care is a right, not a privilege. Jim would have graduated with the UCLA School of Medicine Class of 1984, but he never got the chance. After his death in 1983, the Clinic—now called Saban Community Clinic—established the Jim Slotnick Fellowship in Medicine. The Fellowship, offered every summer, is designed to give UCLA medical students a unique clinical opportunity, where they receive mentoring and hands-on experience providing health care to the underserved at three Saban Community Clinic sites.

Since 1985, thirty UCLA medical students have been selected for the Jim Slotnick Fellowship in Medicine. Most are now physicians around the country, working in specialties ranging from primary care, to emergency medicine, to obstetrics and gynecology, to trauma surgery. Although these Fellows never had the pleasure of meeting

Jim, through their Fellowship they experienced what was most important to him—health care for all, provided with dignity and compassion. Jim's legacy and spirit live on through them.

The Fellows

David Geffen School of Medicine at UCLA

1985—Maria A. Pielaet, MD (Class of 1986)

1986—Richard Sonner, MD (Class of 1987)

1987—Elizabeth (Whaley) McClure, MD (Class of 1989)

1988—David H. Solberg, MD (Class of 1990)

1999—Karen Hutchinson, MD (Class of 1990)

1990—Gilberto Ruiz, MD (Class of 1992)

1992—Gregory B. Seymann, MD (Class of 1994)

1993—Jeanné (Hill) Smith, MD (Class of 1996)

1994—Marie Crandall, MD, MPH, FACS (Class of 1996)

1995—Angel (Hamptonie) Schaffer, MD (Class of 1997)

1996—Samuel M. Tseng, MD (Class of 1998)

1997—Camille Wedlow, MD (Class of 1999)

1998—Jennifer A. Miller, MD, FAAP (Class of 2000)

1999—Lisa Rood, MD (Class of 2001)

2000—Matthew Morrell, MD (Class of 2003)

2001—Seth Cardall, MD (Class of 2004)

2002—Lucas Karaelias, MD (Class of 2005)

2003—Candace J. Jones, MD (Class of 2007)

2004—Christina M. Truong, MD (Class of 2007)

2005—Raymond C. Quon, MD (Class of 2008)

2006—Luu Doan Ireland, MD, MPH (Class of 2009)
2007—Scott I. Lee, MD (Class of 2010)
2008—Joshua W. Elder, MD, MPH (Class of 2012)
2008—Daniel Karlin, MD (Class of 2012)
2009—Carla Spades, MD, MPH (Class of 2013)
2010—Carlos Sandoval, MD, MBA (Class of 2014)
2011—Bo Elizabeth Espinosa-Setchko (Class of 2015)
2012—Monica Boggs (Class of 2016)
2013—Rosibel Hernandez (Class of 2017)
2014—Amy Showen (Class of 2018)
2015—Ricky J. Thomas (Class of 2018)

Saban Community Clinic
(formerly The Los Angeles Free Clinic)

SABAN COMMUNITY CLINIC SERVES AS A MEDICAL home for the underserved and those who are most vulnerable by providing comprehensive, dependable, and affordable quality health care in a caring environment. The Clinic's legacy is rooted in a fundamental belief—health care is a right, not a privilege.

In 1967 the Clinic (originally named the Los Angeles Free Clinic) opened its doors to provide medical and psychological services to low-income and uninsured individuals at no cost. The staff was made up entirely of volunteers and operated solely on donations.

Today the Clinic operates three health centers in Los Angeles County, providing more than 100,000 patient visits to more than 21,000 men, women, and children each year. The Clinic remains committed to keeping its doors open to everyone who needs medical, dental, behavioral healthcare or social services, regardless of ability to pay.

Reflecting its new designation as a Federally Qualified Health Center in a new era in health care with the Patient Protection and Affordable Care Act, the Clinic was renamed Saban Community Clinic in 2013.

For more information visit the Clinic in person or online at: www.sabancommunityclinic.org.

Acknowledgments

Every year for the past twenty-five years, I have gone to Kinko's to make a copy of *A Short Life* to give to the new Jim Slotnick Fellow. I've wanted each of them to have a sense of Jim, the actual person behind the Fellowship. As a result, there must be close to fifty typed, hand-copied, and clunky bound versions of *A Short Life* circulating among Fellows, friends, and family.

Over the years, many people have urged me to publish *A Short Life*. But there were always reasons to keep this from happening. This past year, however, it all fell into place due to the magical efforts of so many people.

This is my chance to thank those people—friends and colleagues, who from the beginning and then all along the way, lent support, encouragement, and hours of their time. You opened doors, guided the path, and most importantly, believed that Jim's story needed to be told.

A Short Life came to be published because of you:

First to Beth Lieberman—for your wisdom, guidance, editing, and shepherding. You did it with heart and understanding, all the while preserving Jim's voice throughout the process of bringing his words to the printed page.

Acknowledgments

To Jon Slotnick, Sara Slotnick, and Ellen Iverson—partners and collaborators from the get-go . . . for your encouragement, your constant support, insight, editing, and friendship.

To Dr. Tinh Vuong—for your steady compassionate presence, and wisdom, and for the initial push to make this book a reality.

To Joshua Elder, MD, and Daniel Karlin, MD—for believing in *A Short Life* as young medical students, and working to bring it to others. Your continued passion and dedication has been inspiring, and your thoughtful and wise notes, your perspective, and your generous open hearts have been invaluable in the process.

To Rosi Hernandez and Monica Boggs—for your time, dedication, insight, thoughtful feedback, as well as your care for *A Short Life*.

To Daniel Butler, MD—for your perspective, candor and willingness to assist.

To my friends and colleagues at Saban Community Clinic with much gratitude—Allyn Cioban, Debbie Fogelman, Lenna Poulatian, Jeff Bujer, Ursula Baffigo, and Christianne Ray. Thank you so much for your time, support and help all along the way.

To my friends and colleagues at UCLA—at the David Geffen School of Medicine—Meredith Szumski and Dahlia Warman, for your support, guidance, and caring for this project. . . . I have so much appreciation for all that you've done; and thank you to Guy Adams from Academic Publishing for your time and kind assistance.

And to those who helped me navigate *A Short Life* along the publishing road...with advice, encouragement, counsel, walks, coffee, laughs, and slow, deep breaths...Wendy Mogel, Amy Wilentz, Taly Ginsberg, Shifra Bemis, Susan Pearlman, Izzy Eichenstein, Wendy Miller, Donald Case...thank you all from my heart.

To those folks who planted the seed way back when...when I didn't even know that seeds were being planted—Michael Wilkes, MD; Susan Mandel, MD; Jehni Robinson, MD; Mark Benor, MD; Brian Prestwich, MD; Noah Craft, MD.

To Don Spetner, my loving and supportive partner, backer, reader, writer, cheerleader. I am so grateful for your presence along every step of the way. I could never have published Jim's book without your deep understsanding and knowing, all the way back from our first connection.

To Jim's mom, Penina Slotnick, in loving memory— for having the vision of publishing Jim's memoir and for making the Jim Slotnick Fellowship a reality.

To Paul Serchia, in loving memory—for holding *A Short Life* near to you and blogging about it.

To Eric Cohen, MD, in loving memory—for being there with Jim at the end, and for carrying on Jim's legacy through your gifted teaching.

And finally, to Jim, for teaching me about loving, living, and dying.

Laurie Goodman, Publisher
Elm Drive Press